The

# LEADERSHIP

## CONNECTION

The Link Between Leading and Succeeding

ERIK THERWANGER

The
# LEADERSHIP
## CONNECTION

The Link Between Leading and Succeeding

Published in Prior Lake, Minnesota, by Think GREAT® LLC


The Leadership CONNECTION™ is a trademark of Think GREAT® LLC

Think GREAT® is a registered trademark of Think GREAT® LLC


ISBN  978-0-9844611-5-8


Library of Congress Subject Headings:

Leadership / Personal Growth / Success


BISAC Subject Headings:

SEL027000    Leadership / Personal Growth / Success


TG_TLC_Bookv01ET – 08-01-2014

## Dedication

This book is dedicated to the United States Marine Corps: the single greatest example of leadership I have ever experienced in my life. And to the Marines I have been blessed to train with, to follow, and to lead. Your commitment to making the leadership connection will always be the hallmark of my personal and professional life.

# CONTENTS

# INTRODUCTION

## MAKE THE DECISION TO LEAD

*Your Position Does Not Make You a Leader.*

The art of leading people has been studied throughout history. But in today's fast-paced environment, most leaders are thrust into leadership positions with little to no training on how to effectively lead others. Countless theories exist, thousands of books have been written, and people pay top-dollar to learn highly valued leadership skills at seminars. In fact, businesses invest hundreds of millions of dollars to train their teams to become better leaders. Why so much focus on leadership? It's simple; success is directly linked to leadership.

With the click of a mouse, you can find virtually every available resource on this life-changing topic. If you searched Google, like I just did, you would find 409,000,000 results. Yes, *409 million*. That's a lot of information to sift through. Perhaps you are looking to order some leadership materials like: books, videos, or audio resources. Let's take a look at Amazon and see what resources you can find. Click ... 104,000 leadership results!

Leadership is a huge topic; one that can be a bit overwhelming and perhaps intimidating. It is often misunderstood, underutilized, and ineffectively implemented. But it is also the single most important factor to your success, the success of your team, and ultimately, the success of your organization. There is no doubt that improving your leadership skills, and the leadership skills of those on your team, will help you to achieve greater results. But where do you start?

Effectively leading your team will make the difference between winning and losing, between succeeding and failing. Every organization can benefit from this common denominator. Unfortunately, most fail to allocate the time and resources needed to develop the leaders on their teams. Yet the cost of building leadership is miniscule compared to the value it brings.

When I launched my company, Think GREAT, I had a simple goal: to translate my personal experiences into meaningful books and powerful presentations that would help people to achieve greater results in their lives. Over a five-year time span, I authored three books: *The GOAL Formula*, *3-D Sales*, and *The SCALE Factor*. I also became a professional speaker, and have been hired to train individuals, teams, and organizations on the concepts in these books.

As a personal development coach, I enjoy helping people to set and accomplish goals (*The GOAL Formula*), to enhance their sales performance (*3-D Sales*), and to improve their health and fitness (*The SCALE Factor*). But the topic I am most requested to train on is ... you guessed it, leadership.

I have had the privilege of working with thousands of team members, sales professionals, executives, and business owners. My presentations have been requested from companies such as Sam's Club, charity organizations including the American Cancer Society, and branches of the armed services like, the United States Marine Corps – three vastly different organizations.

Sam's Club is a Fortune 500 company, The American Cancer Society is one of the largest cancer-fundraisers in the world, and the United States Marine Corps is the most elite fighting force in the world (in my humble opinion). Although these three entities serve tremendously different purposes, they all share a common objective. Each organization wants to achieve greater results; they want to succeed. And to do that, they focus on developing their leaders.

As most people quickly discover, merely assuming a leadership position does not guarantee you will become an effective leader. As leaders, we have many roles. We are morale boosters, problem solvers, goal setters, and strategic planners. We are counselors, therapists, coaches, and cheerleaders all rolled into one. We organize meetings, resolve conflicts, and attempt to keep everyone productive (and happy). In addition to those duties, we still have our own job descriptions to fulfill. Keeping all of those "leadership" plates spinning can be a heavy burden, and that is without facing any personal challenges.

Another thing to consider is that you are typically responsible for continued growth within your team, department, and your entire organization. Leadership is not easy, but it is simple. The good news is that most leaders are fully capable of accomplishing all that is expected of them, and more. The bad news is that they lack the strategies and techniques necessary for making the link between leading and succeeding. This is my specialty. I help leaders, and the members of their teams, to exceed their potential by making *The LEADERSHIP Connection*.

Although I have embraced my role as a leader in every position I have held, there was a starting point for my leadership journey. Three weeks after turning eighteen, I experienced a defining moment that forever changed my perception of what it means to be a leader.

## MY FIRST FULL-TIME JOB

It was the summer of 1987, and I had just graduated from high school. I had been working some part-time, under-the-table jobs, to earn a little cash. Cleaning buses, mowing lawns, and doing small projects provided me some spending money, but I was ready to do something greater with my life. I had made the decision to head in a new direction, and was about to start my first full-time job. As you can imagine, I was a little nervous.

On August 24, 1987, my name became Recruit Therwanger as I exited the bus and entered basic training for the United States Marine Corps. Over the next ninety days, the young men in Platoon 1095 would be transformed from undisciplined civilians into hard-charging Marines.

Our transformation into "The Few and The Proud" did not occur by stepping into camouflage uniforms, shaving our heads, or doing countless push-ups. We did all of that, and much more. But I quickly learned that becoming a Marine was about becoming a leader. For the next three months, our platoon would be in the constant presence of dedicated, passionate, and very loud Marine Corps leaders.

Our four drill instructors were intense, laser-focused, and fully committed to helping us to accomplish our goal: earning the title of U.S. Marine. They embodied the essence of leadership and taught us the traits and principles that were expected of all Marines. Graduating from boot camp and becoming a Marine was not just the end of my basic training, it was the beginning of my life-long leadership journey.

In 1991, as the First Gulf War ended, so did my tour of duty. I was honorably discharged from the Marine Corps. Corporal Therwanger became Erik again. Although I might have packed away my uniforms, I would forever keep with me the leadership skills I developed as a Marine. I had been surrounded by an uplifting leadership culture; one that guided my actions, helped me to overcome obstacles, and was my support during four years of service.

Now it was time to apply what I had learned to my new life. But the level of leadership I had grown accustomed to was hard to find in the civilian sector. Gone was the intense focus of my drill instructors, the unique perspectives of my Staff Non Commissioned Officers (NCOs), and the direct guidance of my officers.

Because my goals and dreams were of the utmost importance, I made the choice to apply the leadership skills I had learned in the Marine Corps to every facet of my new direction in life. I made the decision to lead, and it helped me to stay the course as I pursued all of my goals. Whether I was studying in a university classroom, or making a presentation in an executive board room, my leadership training gave me unbreakable strength.

In business, a lack of leadership can cost money. But in combat, it can cost lives. Although I have spent far more time in a suit and tie than I have in a camouflage uniform, the leadership training I received from the Marine Corps has provided me an unparalleled edge in the business world. Now, you can use that edge to gain distinct advantages in your career and in your life.

## *MAKING THE LEADERSHIP CONNECTION*

Most leaders want to experience the benefits of leadership, but struggle to properly implement it into their organizations. As a trainer, I work closely with all levels of leaders. I coach those who are new to leadership, and I mentor experienced leaders. I train supervisors, managers, executives, military commanders, and business owners.

Leaders struggle because they do not understand how to link together the *Elite Purposes* of a leader. You would likely agree that each position in your organization should serve a specific purpose. Typically, team members who fulfill those positions help an organization to *survive*. They complete the tasks needed to ensure that the organization moves forward.

But more importantly, I believe each leadership position serves elite purposes. A leader should help an organization to thrive and to accomplish the goals necessary to ensure that the organization moves upward.

*The LEADERSHIP Connection* will help your organization to succeed by explaining how to successfully link together the following:

**The Four Elite Purposes (EPs) of a Leader**:

1. **E**nhance **P**erceptions
2. **E**levate **P**riorities
3. **E**mpower **P**eople
4. **E**xceed **P**ossibilities

If you are ready to experience new levels of success, then it is time to make leadership the foundation in your organization. Imagine how it will feel as you make this connection in your company. Imagine what your results would be like as you and your team begin to make *The LEADERSHIP Connection*.

Earlier, when I mentioned that leadership was a huge topic, I asked the question, "Where do you start?" Your leadership journey does not begin when you are appointed to your position. It begins when you make the decision to lead. *The LEADERSHIP Connection* is much more than just a starting point. It will be your guide to making the link between leading and succeeding.

This book is the culmination of my unique experiences as a leader, spanning nearly three decades. I have had the opportunity to flex my leadership muscles as a shift supervisor, a facility manager, a branch office manager, and as an executive business leader. In fact, it was the leadership principles in this book that allowed me to rise from an entry-level job to the position of vice president, while working at a post-production company in the entertainment industry.

I earned the title of VP in less than eighteen months from the day I was hired because my main focus was leading. I developed the leaders around me, launched a dedicated and focused sales team, and helped to create a corporate culture that allowed for many areas of success, including the growth of our annual revenue by over 300 percent. But it all started with leadership.

As you make *The LEADERSHIP Connection*, you will discover that the benefits of leadership do not end at your office door. They positively magnify your entire life. In addition to all of the professional growth you will experience, you will also find your personal life will be forever enriched.

*The LEADERSHIP Connection* will be your road map to developing your leadership skills and transforming your organization into a cohesive team of leaders, capable of accomplishing all objectives. Starting today, the choice is yours to make *The LEADERSHIP Connection*!

*Think GREAT,*

*Erik*

# PART I

## ENHANCE PERCEPTIONS

# PART I

## ENHANCE PERCEPTIONS

*Is Your Leadership Glass Half Empty or Half Full?*

Have you ever made an exciting announcement to your team and their response was less than enthusiastic? If so, you are not alone. Leaders often roll out dynamic changes, inspiring plans, and motivational messages to their teams, only to be met with the resounding sound of ... silence. What went wrong? You were excited. They should be excited too, right?

For a brief moment you think it might be your delivery, or even your timing. But deep inside, you know it was something else. Ultimately, what you *perceived* to be amazing was not *seen* the same way by your audience. When the perceptions of your team fail to align with your own vision, the outcome of such a mismatch can have a devastating impact on your desired results.

Leaders are often left feeling discouraged, frustrated, and sometimes a bit angered by the lack of enthusiasm from their team members. On the other hand, team members are often unimpressed, negative, and sometimes a bit disappointed by the message they receive from their leaders. A definitive "connection" failed to be made.

When the perceptions of the team and the leaders are not connected, or worse yet, the perceptions of the individual leaders are not aligned, you cannot expect to achieve greater results in your organization. Perhaps you are thinking, "Enhancing someone's perception can be a challenging task." Welcome to leadership. Here is some good news ... the ball is in your court! Proven strategies and techniques exist to significantly enhance the perceptions of your team.

Every team member views things differently: policies and procedures, their job duties, the responsibilities of others, workflow, management, the organization's goals, the challenges facing them, and even the contents of what needs to be in the vending machine, just to name a few. The list could go on and on. But no matter how long the list is, their perceptions will affect the way they see you as a leader and how they work toward your organization's common goals.

The ability to understand your team's mindset is challenging enough. But as a leader, you must strive to enhance their perceptions in order to unify your team and position your organization for success. Even though people might see the same thing, they can perceive it differently. There is a huge difference between these two words.

**Seeing**: the physical ability for our brains to translate the data that enters our eyes and transform it into "images" so we can **interpret our environment**.

**Perceiving**: the mental ability for our brains to translate the data that enters our minds and transform it into "meaning" so we can **interpret our circumstances**.

As a leader, the environment you help to create in your organization is critical for your team to perform their duties. But your ability to connect with them and enhance their perceptions, will allow them to conquer their circumstances, paving the way for continued growth and success. As a leader, that is what you are striving for, isn't it? Continued growth and success?

Enhancing the perceptions of team members and other leaders is an all-the-time responsibility. But how do you influence people to look at things differently, and to perceive a win-win perspective? Developing your team and growing your organization is like building a great structure. You cannot expect it to remain standing when it has been built upon a weak foundation.

Unfortunately, many leaders attempt to do just that. They have visions of their "building" stretching into the skies and producing great results, but they spend very little time working on strengthening the foundation needed to support it all. What makes up the foundation of your organization? If you were building a home, would it be worth your time to focus on building a strong foundation before you start putting up the walls? Absolutely.

## BUILDING A STRONG FOUNDATION

Typically, you will not need to wear a hard hat while making *The LEADERSHIP Connection* at your organization. But understanding why building contractors start with a solid foundation for their buildings will provide great insight for leaders who strive to build and develop their organizations.

A solid foundation is designed to hold up and keep together the structure above it. A building built only on bare earth is more likely to become cracked and damaged over time. Furthermore, the ground is never quite still and in many cases not totally solid. A strong foundation increases the longevity of the building, and ensures that it remains safer for the people inside of it.

The foundation of a building requires three critical elements to increase its strength: cement, sand, and water. The proper mixture of these elements creates concrete, which has been instrumental in creating structures such as the Hoover Dam and even the Coliseum of ancient Rome, which is still standing, nearly 2,000 years later.

As a leader, the foundation (enhanced perceptions) you are establishing will help you to elevate priorities, empower people, and exceed possibilities in your organization. Similar to any given structure, each organization faces its own natural hazards, which can have a negative impact on your "building."

The egos, attitudes, and varying personalities of your team can take their toll, unless you create a strong foundation by enhancing their perceptions. To do this, you will need to combine three critical elements: a leadership definition, a unifying culture, and important goals.

**The Three Elements for a Strong Foundation:**

1.  Clearly Define Leadership

2.  Develop a Unifying Culture

3.  Identify Important Goals

Most leaders struggle to understand why their team members are reluctant to help them build a better company. It is usually not that people have a lack of belief in the new direction, but rather a lack of faith in the old foundation. If you want the "buy-in" from your team, harness the power of creating a strong foundation to help enhance their perceptions.

By paying particular attention to enhancing the perceptions of your team, you will establish a higher level of confidence, stability, and dedication. Communicating the deeper meaning of leadership, culture, and goals will significantly enhance your ability to achieve greater results.

## IT ALL STARTS WITH THE LEADERS

People assigned to leadership positions typically possess a solid understanding of the products, services, and unique workflow of their organizations. But to succeed as a leader, you will need much more than a knowledge of how the company functions. You must possess a deeper understanding of how to enhance the perceptions of your team.

When I train leaders, I use a highly effective, state-of-the-art training tool – a 3x5 card. My corporate training sessions often begin by having the leaders in the room take a few minutes to clearly articulate three things for me. On the small blank card, they jot down their own definition of leadership, a brief description of the organization's culture, and the current goals of the company.

I give them only a minute to compile their thoughts, and as you might have already guessed, I receive a wide variety of answers. Many leaders struggle to articulate these three vital components. If a leader is unable to explain the foundation of their organization, why would anyone stand on it? Or stand for it?

If leaders cannot define "leadership," how can they effectively guide their team? They cannot! What happens if a leader struggles to describe the culture within the company, or worse yet, there is no discernible culture? Without a unifying culture, the team will experience a lack of identity, which often produces a lack of commitment.

Last but not least, I encounter leaders, who are on a "leadership" team, but do not fully understand their organization's goals. Goals provide hope and give inspiration. They set a clear direction for the entire team. When a leader does not know the destination, how can anyone be expected to arrive there?

**Leadership Link**  Take a 3x5 card and jot down your own definition of leadership, a brief description of your organization's culture, and the current goals of your company. For added impact, have each of your leaders do it too.

Imagine how much more confident you will feel as a leader as you clearly define leadership, develop a unifying culture, and identify the important goals within your organization. Now, imagine how inspired your team will be to know that the foundation of your organization is strong, solid, and ready for growth.

As a leader, the meaning behind your message is paramount. "Why" you are doing something is usually far more important than "what" you are doing. By focusing on leadership, culture, and goals, your confidence and certainty will grow, and soon you will begin to enhance the perceptions of your team members and other leaders.

As you announce new plans and roll out new initiatives, silence will be replaced by the sound of a unified and excited team – a team ready to follow their leader.

Always keep in mind that most people want to be a part of something great, something special, and something life-changing. Leaders ensure that their team members know the organization is moving in that direction, and being built on a solid foundation.

Only by enhancing the perceptions of the team will leaders create a shared vision within their organization. Your success as a leader will ultimately rest on your ability to change the way your team views their circumstances, not just their environments. To start enhancing perceptions, let's take a closer look at defining leadership for your organization.

# CHAPTER 1

## CLEARLY DEFINE LEADERSHIP

### What Does it Mean to be a Leader?

What are some important elements to a successful marriage? Among many others, you would probably agree that love, trust, desire, respect, compassion, friendship, communication, and fidelity should be at the top of the list. What could happen if two people fell in love, married, but then discovered they had different definitions of what each of those words meant? What impact would it have on their relationship? Sadly, statistics show that over 50 percent of marriages will end in divorce.

While many factors could end a marriage, I believe most relationships begin to erode because the two people, who were once head-over-heels in love with each other, did not share the same definition of what it means to be married. Most relationships begin with high levels of excitement and passion, but all of that can quickly fall apart if important aspects of their marriage are left open for interpretation.

When definitions are misunderstood, or worse yet, never established, the outcome is rarely positive. As a leader, the relationships you develop are paramount to your success. Inaccurate definitions can negatively affect your team, your peers, your leaders, your vendors, and your customers. You cannot afford to have important aspects of your business interpreted incorrectly. Yet many leaders only hope their team shares the same definitions for important concepts. But *hope* is not a solid strategy for leaders.

The most important word you can define for your organization is "leadership." When I review the 3x5 cards from my training sessions, I am amazed at the high level of variance in the definitions of this critical element. From junior leaders to senior executives, the meaning dramatically differs. No wonder individual members on the same leadership team often experience a wide array of varying results.

For a team to accomplish its objectives, the leaders must develop a shared meaning of leadership and what it means to be a leader in their organization. But creating a definition can be a difficult task. Did you know that the Oxford English Dictionary currently contains 171,476 words? While we only use a small portion of these words on a daily basis, each one can have many different definitions. "Leadership" is no different. It has numerous meanings and perceptions.

It is imperative that leaders create their own unique interpretation of the word; one that will unify both the leaders and the team. Just as a marriage can begin to dissolve because of misunderstandings, many leaders experience a similar deterioration with their professional relationships by failing to establish a shared and consistent definition of leadership.

## DEFINING LEADERSHIP FOR YOUR TEAM

Leadership tends to have two distinct perspectives in most organizations. First is the perception of those doing the leading, and second, the perception of those being led. If you think the answers on the 3x5 cards, given by the leaders, have some head-scratching definitions, try asking employees to describe the level of leadership they are receiving. Make sure you give each of them more than one card because they usually have no shortage of constructive feedback about their leaders.

The importance of defining leadership in your company does not only help to support the current leaders, it benefits the entire team. Because the ability to accomplish your goals will be based on the combined efforts of the team members and the leaders, you must connect them all with a shared definition of leadership.

In its most basic form, "leadership" can be defined as, "the position or office of a leader." Being said, we are all in a position of leadership. But that does not mean we all effectively lead our teams. This definition simply implies we have been appointed to a position requiring a leader. So the big question becomes, "What is a leader?"

Many might hold the title, but most do not fully understand the importance of what it means to lead people. Without a solid definition in place, you will fail to make the connection with your team, your leaders, and any other important relationships. Depending on who you speak with, the word "leader" can have a number of different meanings.

- To a fisherman, a *leader* means: a short length of wire, or similar material by which a hook is attached to a fishing line.

- To a film editor, a *leader* means: a blank strip at the beginning or end of a film, used in threading or winding.

- To a plumber, a *leader* means: the section of a storm drain that guides water away from a roof.

All of these unique definitions are correct, especially if you fish, edit films, or install storm drains. But they will not help you to effectively lead your team and achieve the desired results you seek. To do so, you will need a meaningful, purpose-filled definition of what it means to be a leader in your organization.

I have spent years developing my own personal definition of what I expect of myself as a leader. I keep it simple, direct, and free of misunderstandings. It is based on the concepts I learned in the Marine Corps, the skills I personally applied in the business sector, and the strategies I have successfully shared with thousands of leaders across the country. My definition constantly holds me to a higher standard. Your definition should, too.

To me, the word "lead" implies movement in a specified direction. So you must have a clear vision of your desired destination. After all, as a leader you are going somewhere, right? The word "leader" suggests that people are following you, or at least they *should* be following you. So where are you leading them? In addition to articulating the destination, you must clearly express what it will take for your team to arrive there.

My definition of being a leader helps to energize and keep me focused. It inspires me to continually grow. There are many traits, skills, theories, philosophies, techniques, and strategies about leading. But there is only one definition I use to distinguish myself as a leader.

***Think GREAT Leader***: a person who clearly outlines a specified destination, and guides people there by course-correcting and adhering to the greater purpose behind the goals necessary for success.

**Leadership Link**  Write your definition of what it means to be a leader. Create your own unique version, borrow parts from mine, or use my entire definition. Most importantly, fully embrace it.

Establishing what it means to be a leader is an exciting process. No longer are you looking to merely fill positions, you are seeking to fulfill expectations on a journey to greatness. You will be able to identify up-and-coming leaders on your team, and then create an environment of internal growth and personal development.

## *LEADERS LEAVE A LASTING IMPRESSION*

Great leaders always leave a lasting impression on the people they lead. In a leadership position, it is far easier to leave a negative impression than a positive one. As a leader, you are constantly under the microscope. Every action you take and every word you speak is closely scrutinized, analyzed, and interpreted.

Over twenty years later, I can still recall specific moments when my drill instructors enhanced my perception of "why" we were doing specific tasks. The physical training in boot camp was very demanding, but our leaders consistently expressed the greater purpose behind our actions. Before we began any physical activity, we were instructed to repeat, "The more we sweat in peace, the less we bleed in war." A perception-changing statement indeed.

No longer was I merely climbing over obstacles, running for miles, or performing endless calisthenics, I was working on improving my chances for survival in combat. My tasks took on a different meaning because my leaders pointed out the bigger picture involved – staying alive! They left a lasting impression on me and the recruits of Platoon 1095.

Defining what it means to be a leader in your organization is a powerful start. But to experience the benefits of this process, you and your leaders will need to understand and adopt the traits that make a leader great.

## THE TRAITS OF A GREAT LEADER

Although some people seem more natural at it, no one is born with leadership skills. Like everything else, leadership is a learned behavior. Many people are appointed to a leadership position, but do not possess the traits to lead. When leadership is nothing more than a title, very little can be achieved.

A good marriage might start by defining words such as love, respect, and fidelity. But a great marriage is experienced only when the qualities of both people meet their defined expectations. When someone fails to live up to these expectations, relationships dramatically suffer.

The qualities of a leader are always revealed through the traits they display. And their traits are quickly exhibited by what they say and what they do. Using the right leadership traits will help you to leave a lasting impression on the people you lead, and to ensure you will achieve your desired results.

Your traits should embody your definition of leadership, allowing you to inspire, motivate, and move your team. But what is a trait? A trait is a distinguishing feature of a person's character. Through words and actions, traits reveal who a person truly is. Each time you communicate and every time you take an action, you show your traits. A leader's character is always on display.

There is no such thing as a leader without challenges. But we are not defined by our difficult circumstances. We are however, defined by how we respond to those challenges. The qualities of a leader must be in alignment with the traits expected of great leaders.

Many organizations fail to identify the traits they expect of their leadership team, forcing some leaders to rely on their "good" intentions to navigate through challenging circumstances. The intentions of a leader last but a moment, but their words and actions will leave a permanent impression, positive or negative, on everyone they encounter.

How important are the words and actions of a leader? They are of great importance, so let's take a look at the traits that will help you to shine. To do that, we are going to examine the fourteen Leadership Traits of the U.S. Marine Corps.

## 14 LEADERSHIP TRAITS OF THE U.S. MARINE CORPS

Accepting a leadership position should be an exciting time. But it can also be a stressful experience. Most leaders are left to their own devices when it comes to establishing the "leadership" components of their position. New leaders might look to their new job description to gain an understanding of what is expected, but these documents tend to outline their job duties, not their leadership expectations.

Since 1775, The Marine Corps has overcome insurmountable odds, endured great challenges, and survived life-threatening situations. They have done so in an ever-changing environment, and their leaders have successfully led their Marines through every conflict our country has faced; from the American Revolutionary War to the War on Terror.

The Marine Corps attributes their success to the leadership skills of their Marines and they have dedicated their time and resources to help the men and women in their ranks to apply fourteen specific traits.

I was introduced to these fourteen traits as a raw recruit in boot camp. Before my training was complete; before I learned how to fire my rifle; before I earned the title of U.S. Marine, I studied these concepts then, and still do today.

In typical Marine Corps fashion, the use an acronym to identify, and help us to remember, these important traits: JJ DID TIE BUCKLE

## JJ DID TIE BUCKLE

1. Justice — Being fair and consistent.
2. Judgment — Making the right decisions.
3. Dependability — Your team should be able to rely on you.
4. Initiative — Taking action, even without orders.
5. Decisiveness — Make decisions without delay.
6. Tact — How you treat people.
7. Integrity — Be honest and truthful in what you say and do.
8. Enthusiasm — Have a sincere interest in your duties.
9. Bearing — The way you conduct and carry yourself.
10. Unselfishness — Put the team above yourself. Give credit to others.
11. Courage — Remaining calm while recognizing fear.
12. Knowledge — Know your job, your team, and current events.
13. Loyalty — Possess an unwavering devotion to your team.
14. Endurance — The mental and physical stamina to stay on course.

Imagine what your leaders could accomplish as they adopt these traits. Imagine the impact on your entire team; your entire organization. Like me, you probably get a sense of excitement and newfound hope just by reading them. Wait until you apply them.

Keep in mind that no one is 100 percent perfect on each of these traits. Constantly strive to be better and continually encourage your team to embrace these traits. You now have parameters to hold yourself and other leaders to a higher level.

**Leadership Link** Have your leaders (yourself included) write down each of the 14 leadership traits and rank themselves on a scale of 1-10 (10 being best). Next, have them rank themselves from their team's perspective. How would they rank their leaders? Discuss ways to improve each ranking.

By clearly defining what it means to be a leader in your organization, you will provide your leaders with a definitive understanding of their leadership role. Then, as you identify the traits expected of a leader, you will provide them with a substantial tool for setting and maintaining the highest levels of personal excellence within your organization.

Clearly defining leadership is the first step to *Enhancing Perceptions*.

# CHAPTER 2

## DEVELOP A UNIFYING CULTURE

Culture Follows the Leader.

Over the past twenty years, corporate *culture* has become an increasingly popular buzz phrase, with many leaders attributing their success to the benefits of creating and operating within a dynamic environment. The importance of culture cannot be understated, but it is often overlooked. Many leaders pay far too little attention to the impact their organization's culture has on their results.

Developing a unifying culture will help you to influence your leaders and your team members in many ways. But before you rush off to reap the benefits of a strong culture, let's first understand what a culture is and what it will do for your organization.

As you already know, every word has many meanings. Culture is no different, and while most leaders fail to define it, others tend to accept the already-established culture within their organizations. Worse yet, some ignore it altogether. Like a block of clay, leaders must pay particular attention to their role in continually shaping, molding, and strengthening their culture.

Webster's dictionary defines culture as "a way of thinking, behaving, or working that exists in a place or organization." An organization's culture is its model or style of operating. It creates the mood of the company, and determines how people communicate with one another and work toward accomplishing goals together. Culture impacts every person who encounters it.

Why is culture so important to an organization? Because it has the ability to pull people together, to provide them with inner fortitude, and to build camaraderie. Most importantly, it has the power to enhance their perceptions. With an inspiring environment in place, team members will see the impossible as possible. They will develop a "can-do" attitude, and they will concentrate on the solutions for success, rather than dwell on the obstacles of failure.

When you set out to accomplish your organization's goals (Chapter 3), would you rather entrust them to a team operating in a strong environment or a weak one? Successful leaders accomplish goals, and behind every successful leader is a culture filled with energy, excitement, and enthusiasm.

## CULTURE MATTERS

Before business leaders ever attempted to develop corporate cultures, human beings have relied on their societies to help create unique identities, to bond people together, and to provide the standard behavior for people to follow. Culture links people together on a much deeper level than a paycheck ever will.

The essence of culture is people, not profits. Too many business leaders attempt to capitalize on the benefits of incorporating culture into their organizations, but they rarely realize why culture truly matters. When you implement a culture only to increase your results, you will struggle. But when you develop a culture that unifies the members of your team, you will more easily achieve your desired results, and open the door to new opportunities.

One of the first things that became apparent when I enlisted in the Marine Corps, was the unbreakable bond these warriors share. I quickly noticed the high level of culture each Marine embraces; unified with core values and traditions that have been passed down from Marine to Marine for over two hundred years.

While each branch of our Armed Services have their own unique cultures, the Marines use a simple phrase to sum up their devotion and loyalty: *esprit de corps*. "The Spirit of the Corps" embodies their deep regard for history, traditions, and honor that allows each Marine to operate as an integral part of a cohesive unit. The culture of the Marine Corps is based on their people. What is your environment based on?

Developing a unifying culture is a formidable task, and there is no single formula for success. As a leader, one of the most important aspects of creating this type of environment is to encourage team members to embrace new ways of thinking; new ways of working together. Inevitably, an organization's goals will evolve from year to year, and leaders must ensure that their teams adapt and grow to meet the needs of those changes.

Regardless of what products and services your organization offers, remember you are in the people business, and culture is based on people. Corporate environments should not focus solely on policies, procedures, or even profits. It should emphasize values, principles, and character. This is what develops a unifying culture.

## ASSESSING YOUR ENVIRONMENT

Successful leaders keep their fingers on the pulse of their culture because a discouraging culture can do a significant amount of damage to an organization. Signs of a lackluster environment can include:

1.  No shared values
2.  Lack of trust
3.  A focus on the problems
4.  Failures are tolerated
5.  People are not enjoying their work

When a negative culture is able to take hold, people lose confidence in their team and in their leaders. This type of environment will make your job as leader exponentially more challenging and will push you and your team further away from your goals. Assessing your culture, and making the necessary course corrections, is critical to your success.

An organization's environment is comprised of many components; everything from dress code to room decor, and from paid vacations to performance reviews. When formulating their feelings about their environment, team members reflect on a wide array of elements.

What indicators should you monitor to gain a better understanding of your culture? While many methods are used to assess the status of an organization's environment, three main techniques are commonly used, but each has its limitations.

1. Historical data

2. Surveys

3. Observations

Historical data can be helpful in that it can show trends in employee absenteeism, performance, and turnover. It can also display customer relations, retention, and satisfaction. It could be fair to say an organization with high employee turnover does not have an inspiring culture. But that is not always the case. The Marine Corps has a 64 percent turnover rate every four years, but their environment is so strong that Marines continue to uphold it even after their tour of duty is complete.

On the other hand, I have worked with many companies with long-term team members, but their culture is dismal. Some people stay on board for a paycheck – not for passion. While helpful, historical data might or might not accurately depict your environment.

Surveys can also be beneficial, provided that the feedback you receive is truthful. Many team members do not express their real feelings, especially when they know their leaders will be privy to the information. In addition, most surveys tend to have set questions with set answers, not allowing the person taking the survey to pick a response that accurately represents how they truly feel about the question. While providing some insight, surveys can be perceived as impersonal.

While observation is probably the most effective of the three, team members will more than likely behave at their best when they are being observed, especially by their leaders. Observation can provide you with valuable information about your culture, but it might not reflect the entire truth.

I have used all three techniques, but found one particular method provided me with the information I truly needed to assess the environment properly and make the necessary enhancements to develop a unifying culture: personal interaction.

In Shakespeare's "Henry V," King Henry shed his royal attire and walked among his troops during the early morning. With the approaching battle of Agincourt just hours away, Henry goes in disguise and joins four ordinary soldiers as they sit around a fire. Facing near certain death, the men voice their concerns – not just about dying, but about King Henry's leadership.

It was here that Henry exhibited a powerful leadership skill in gathering valuable information about his culture. He listened. He went on to deliver one of the longest soliloquies that Shakespeare had ever written. Ultimately, Henry connects himself and his troops to his core values, and he changed their perception. He was victorious as a soldier and a leader.

While I do not recommend you go in disguise to discover the truth from your team members, I do emphasize that leadership is a people business and leaders need to spend more time with their people. Too many leaders talk to their team members only when something goes wrong. Look for opportunities to talk with them about what they are doing right, and invest the time necessary to build their trust and improve your culture.

As you open up lines of communication, your team will share the important information you need to know about your environment, from a point of view you might not often see. I attained my most valuable information over lunches and coffees, typically out of the office. Investing the necessary one-on-one time with your team will provide a huge return.

## *ENHANCING YOUR CULTURE*

Assessing culture is one thing; enhancing it is another. It takes time, patience, and persistency for a leader to shape an organization's environment. While the multiple elements that identify a culture are unique among each organization, some common denominators help to support unifying cultures.

Dress code, room colors, and the lounge amenities might shape people's perceptions, but I have found three distinct components that resonate deeper with every team member and every leader. These elements will help to develop the unifying culture your team needs to succeed. They also help to answer three important questions: why, how, and what.

**The Three Elements of a Unifying Culture:**

1. The Big Picture    – Why?

2. The Style    – How?

3. The Opportunity    – What?

## *THE BIG PICTURE*

Why does your organization do what it does? Is your organization bigger than its products and services? Leaders help to develop and continually share their organization's Big Picture – everything that represents your company, inside and outside.

**Inside**: includes mission and vision statements, core values, and brand statements to help create a unique identity for the team. Successful leaders harness the power of this identity to move the team forward.

- *Mission*: your organization's current purpose – why it exists.

- *Vision*: your organization's future objectives – where it is going.

- *Core Values*: your main principles that support your mission and vision.

- *Brand Statement*: A marketing tool that encompasses your organization's essence and reputation.

Most organizations identify themselves to their team members and customers by using one or more, or a combination, of the above definitions. Ultimately, what you are striving for is to create a "Who" statement. Let people know more of "who" your organization is; who the people are.

A leader ensures that the organization's identity is brought to life and does not end up as mere words on a sheet of paper.

**Outside**: great organizations do great things beyond office walls. They give back to their communities and to the greater good. Serving in the Marine Corps gave me a tremendous sense of pride and self-worth, but not just because of our accomplishment on the battlefields. Marines also help children in their communities.

The Marine Corps launched their famous Toys for Tots program in 1947, and they have collected and delivered over 469,000,000 toys to children since then. This program gives each Marine, and their families, something to take part in for the greater good of their community. It also develops a deeper sense of pride and satisfaction.

As a leader, provide your team with the opportunity to do something greater than fulfill their job descriptions. Provide them with an opportunity to grow outside of your organization as well as inside.

## THE STYLE

*What* your company does is important and *why* it does it is even more important. But *how* it does it speaks volumes about the culture of your organization. The style in which your organization processes business, makes its products, and delivers its services can be summed up as workflow. Workflow involves a team in order to be successful.

I can say from experience that most organizations do not lack the ability to design a proper workflow. They understand what needs to happen at Point A, and what needs to happen at Point B. However, most leaders fall short when it comes to implementing the processes, procedures, and communication required to successfully create a unifying system.

Workflow has the ability to unify departments or build walls between them. It can improve communication among team members or completely silence it. Workflow can improve cooperation or increase resentment. Most people do not leave an organization because they dislike what the company does, they leave because they do not like the way things are done.

Does this sound familiar? "It was operations fault," says the sales team. "It was the sales department's responsibility," cried the operations team. When you have contention between departments, look closely at your workflow, and ensure that your system unifies your team and promotes exceptional communication.

Ultimately, workflow helps to make your company memorable; to your team and to your customers. Every step in a defined workflow needs an individual or department to be held accountable. It requires team members to communicate, and positions leaders to pay greater attention to making sure that all of the gears are turning properly.

## THE OPPORTUNITY

Growth is a crucial component of each organization. Sales growth, customer satisfaction growth, and team growth are all paramount. If a company is not growing, it is dying. Leaders are appointed to help facilitate all areas of growth within their organizations. But the problem is that too many leaders only focus on growth. I know, focusing on growth sounds like a good thing.

While team members might listen to you speak about growth, they are ultimately waiting to hear about the opportunity. What's in it for them? People often leave growing organizations because they feel left out; perceiving that the company benefitted from their efforts, but they did not. Never make the mistake that people should just be happy to have a job. Great leaders constantly find ways to provide incentives, promotions, and enhancement as the organization grows.

**Leadership Link** Successful leaders achieve growth for the company and for their team!

## YOUR CULTURE

Without a defined culture, leaders struggle to maximize their potential as well as the potential of their team members. Simultaneously, they minimize opportunities for the growth of their organization. By focusing on the big picture, the style, and the opportunities available, you will develop a unifying culture that will dramatically increase your results.

As your company grows, a positive, supportive environment will help to keep it on track. It will enable you to retain strong team members, weed out weak ones, and attract new energetic employees for future growth.

When a culture is positive, inspiring, and collaborative, each team member will share a common purpose with the activities required – to help promote growth. Most importantly, a unifying culture will allow the team to experience a sense of dedication and excitement toward accomplishing the goals necessary for success.

# CHAPTER 3

## IDENTIFY IMPORTANT GOALS

*A Leader Without Goals is like a Ship
Without a Rudder.*

The way your team perceives your organization is the way they present your organization; to each other and to your customers. By clearly defining what it means to be a leader (Chapter 1) and developing a unifying culture for your team (Chapter 2), you have already started to enhance their perceptions. One additional component will help you to dramatically change the way people view your company and their role in it.

Many leaders fail to see the value of investing the time necessary to identify important goals for their business. Whether it is the department manager who has too much on his or her plate, the high-level executive with years of experience, or the business owner who believes he or she already has all of the answers, most miss the opportunity of incorporating life-changing goals into their workplace.

Preparing their service members for long deployments, I was invited to share my goal-setting strategies for many commands in the Air National Guard. Understanding the positive impact of setting and accomplishing goals, much of their literature emphasized that their troops and their families set meaningful goals together.

With divorce rates, depression, and suicide rates at critically high levels, I did not take lightly my opportunity to share strategies and techniques that would help our nation's heroes and their families to stay focused on their goals, especially during the most challenging of times.

Leaders have countless excuses why they fail to set important goals, but there is one, rock-solid reason to firmly establish them: they enhance perceptions. How do goals help to enhance perceptions? Important goals give hope, and inspire and promote forward-thinking. They create a common objective which builds camaraderie, loyalty, and teamwork. As you share the Big Picture of your organization with your team, important goals will give them purpose, far beyond their job descriptions.

Every accomplished goal moves you and your team one step closer to the grand vision of your company. Leaders must pay particular attention to developing a culture that will support the accomplishment of the important goals necessary for growth. Remember, leaders guide their teams in a specific direction. The goals you set and accomplish are milestones on the path to the destination. Identify important goals, and then pour resources into the achievement of these vital objectives.

Setting and accomplishing goals are two completely different things. Most organizations fall short in their efforts because they lack a detailed understanding of how and why they need to accomplish important goals in their environment. Understanding three essential elements will dramatically increase your ability to set and accomplish important goals, while simultaneously enhancing the perceptions of your entire team.

**Three Essential Elements of Important Goals:**

1.  The Types

2.  The Effect

3.  The Steps

Important goals are necessary for a business to grow. They are the most effective way to decide how to move forward, and how stay on the right path to achieve greater results. The accomplishment of those goals will help to increase trust, belief levels, and motivation throughout the entire organization. Important goals are much more important than most leaders realize.

## *GOALS ARE NOT TASKS*

I often meet leaders who confuse goals with tasks. In order to accomplish important goals in your organization, many necessary tasks will be associated with them. Tasks make up the individual duties required for accomplishing each of your goals. But there is a significant difference between goals and tasks.

While most people find a sense of satisfaction after a task has been completed, that feeling is usually temporary and quickly fades away. Goals are different. The satisfaction gained from accomplishing a goal is long-lasting, providing inspiration and positive energy. Another significant difference is that you do not have to wait until a goal is accomplished to receive the full benefit. Moving forward with your goals increases the performance and enhances the perceptions of everyone involved.

Leaders are often a bit hesitant about setting important goals for their teams, departments, and organizations. The idea of taking on a project like this can seem daunting, especially when thousands of unique goals could qualify as "important" to an organization's growth. So where do you start?

## *TYPES OF GOALS*

Your perception of goals is the best place to begin. Most leaders use goals as a way to keep their organization alive. But being alive and growing are far different. If your organization needs a monthly revenue of $500,000 to "keep the lights on," then $500,000 might seem like a good goal to hit each month. Most team members look at these goals as unfulfilling quotas.

Important goals, however, help an organization to break beyond the status quo and enable it to move upward, toward greater results. They inspire team members, and encourage them to unleash their true potential. They allow people to see themselves differently.

Important goals give power. They are like the engine of a vehicle, more specifically, a six-piston engine. Why an engine? Because your organization is a vehicle. And that vehicle has been built to move forward, heading in a direction that will arrive at a GREAT destination. Important goals are the pistons of that engine. They provide unlimited sources of power and energy to your team. But to achieve maximum performance, it is crucial that all six pistons operate and fire in unison.

I have had the privilege of collaborating directly with leaders from hundreds of different organizations and industries. Working with each of them has provided me the opportunity to be involved with thousands of unique goals that move their organizations upward.

While the goals themselves might have been slightly different in scope and size, I discovered that virtually every one fell into six categories. To successfully accomplish a goal in one category, make the link between the other five.

## Types of Goals:

1. Financial
2. Customer
3. Team
4. Operational
5. Marketing
6. Community

### FINANCIAL GOALS

- These goals help to assess an organization's performance. Establishing and monitoring measurable financial goals will help to increase earnings and profit margins, while also allowing for more effective budgeting.

- Financial goals can be established based on benchmarking the "best-in-industry" as well as your own organization's historical performance.

- Examples of common financial goals are: increase revenue by 25 percent, improve profit margins by 10 percent, and reduce unnecessary expenses by 5 percent.

- Most organizations tend to focus only on financial goals, feeling that accomplishing these goals will solve all of their problems. Financial goals are only one piston in your engine.

## CUSTOMER GOALS

- These goals help to increase customer retention, expand your customer base through referrals, and improve relationships between team members and customers.

- Customer goals help your organization to measure its progress toward achieving the highest levels of customer satisfaction, which will have a direct impact on the success of your financial goals. Customer goals establish performance standards, and help to develop improvement programs for team members and leaders.

- Examples of common customer goals are: reducing order errors by 50 percent, developing loyalty programs, and establishing consistent communication with the current customer base.

- Accomplishing customer goals will help to influence the customer's perception of your team and your organization.

- Most organizations can immediately identify the customer goals needed to improve their results, but they often fail to implement the company-wide steps necessary to guarantee long-term success.

## TEAM GOALS

- These goals build loyalty, inspire creativity, increase morale, and decrease complaining. Team goals emphasize the "opportunity" that develops from the "growth" of your organization.

- Team goals announce to your staff that they are a priority, not just another cog in the wheel. They also promote high levels of personal and professional development within your organization.

- Examples of important team goals are: setting up financial rewards, establishing educational programs, and opening up more opportunities for promotion.

- Most leaders only consider team goals as a way to raise morale, so their team members perform better. Effective team goals place an emphasis on the personal and professional development of the team.

## OPERATIONAL GOALS

- These goals increase effectiveness and efficiency, by focusing on the improvement of the workflow and communication within your organization. These goals will increase productivity while decreasing mistakes.

- Operational goals are best accomplished by having team members involved in the development, implementation, and maintenance of these necessary objectives.

- Examples of important operational goals are: revising the procedures within your workflow system (checkpoints, order forms, reports), streamlining internal communication, and setting up consistent benchmarks to track the results of your goals. Benchmarks allow you to follow the timeframes needed to complete a transaction, as well as analyzing the type/frequency of errors.

- Most leaders make a significant mistake by failing to set operational goals, robbing themselves of the valuable information needed to make urgent course corrections. They attempt to navigate through the subpar systems already in place, instead of investing the time necessary for accomplishing important operational goals.

- Accomplishing these goals will allow you to improve your chances for hitting your customer goals. Making consistent improvements to the way you do business, will open the door to doing more business.

## MARKETING GOALS

- These goals will increase your social media reach, elevate web traffic, and improve results from advertising campaigns. They create excitement and influence existing customers, as well as potential new customers, to take a closer look at everything your organization has to offer.

- Marketing goals should include the input from your entire team. Their involvement will increase their buy-in and make them feel like an integral part of the organization as it grows and reaches new heights.

- Examples of important marketing goals are: developing or enhancing your mission and vision statements, creating a brand statement, launching a new version of the website, and starting a "contacting campaign" to deliver a new message to customers.

- Most organizations understand the value of important marketing goals, but fail to ever experience their benefits. I believe this is due in part to the perceived expense associated with marketing initiatives. The above-mentioned marketing goals provide a way to enhance your marketing results without investing significant amounts of money.

## COMMUNITY GOALS

- These goals help to leave a lasting impact in the lives of everyone your organizations touches – far more than any product or service ever will.

- Community goals provide your team with a greater sense of purpose, achievement, and fulfillment. Community goals bond team members, leaders, customers, and vendors. They also have the power of introducing to your organization, people who might have never had the opportunity of connecting before.

- Examples of community goals are: raising money for specific charities, creating volunteer teams to participate in community events, and establishing "green" objectives that will have a positive impact on our global environment, such as minimizing the use of paper, within your organization.

- Most organizations do not invest the time necessary to identify important community goals. But the results of these goals might actually create the deepest sense of commitment and loyalty from your team, increasing their desire to help accomplish all of your other goals.

**Leadership**     Challenge yourself to identify at least one goal in each cat-
**Link**           egory that would be important to your organization.

## THE IMPACT OF GOALS

Setting and accomplishing important goals will have a significant impact on the perceptions of your team. Whether that outlook is positive or negative is up to you. Leaders are often dismayed when their staff fails to embrace the important goals that have been set, even when the accomplishment of those goals will provide high levels of corporate growth.

How can the important goals of your organization create a positive impact for your team? I have discovered three ways to ensure that the right impact occurs with each important goal.

### 1.  Enlist the Help of Your Team

I find it ironic that goal setting typically involves only the senior leadership team. But the accomplishment of the important goals that will significantly enhance the results of the organization, fall onto the entire team. I cannot overstate the importance of their involvement in the goal-setting process.

Team members who actively participate in this process are more likely to actively participate in the goal-accomplishing process. Enlisting their help not only increases their buy-in, but team members often provide an insight that can be helpful in the development of important goals.

## 2. Show Your Team the Benefits

Your team members have likely joined your company for a variety of reasons. But their decision to stay, and more importantly, to become a powerful contributor, will be based on the opportunities available to them through the accomplishment of important goals. Successful leaders make the link between the growth of their organization and the benefits for their team.

What important goals do people care most about? Their own! When someone benefits from a goal, he or she takes ownership of that goal. Ultimately, people are motivated by factors that directly and positively impact their careers and personal lives. Great leaders are able to help their teams to accomplish their personal and professional goals as the organization accomplishes its important goals.

## 3. Harness the Power of Teamwork

Important goals unify a team. Team members who work together to accomplish the goals that will benefit their personal lives, will develop a kindred spirit. Shared goals bring people together, and help to build the camaraderie needed, to not only accomplish important goals, but to exceed them.

Co-created goals increase the level of buy-in you receive from your team. By increasing the number of people who will benefit from accomplishing these goals, you will increase the level of teamwork. Highly-motivated team members have a willingness to get the job done efficiently and effectively, creating greater results and higher levels of success.

## *THE STEPS TO ACCOMPLISHING GOALS*

Taking on important goals might seem like a daunting task. People often feel overwhelmed at the thought of the newly required tasks, as well as the additional efforts necessary to ensure each goal is realized. Understanding the steps needed to accomplish each goal is critical. In addition to providing structure and accountability, they will help to balance the energy required for success.

When it comes to accomplishing goals, I could write an entire book on this subject. Wait a minute – I have. As the author of *The GOAL Formula*, I regularly share the strategies and techniques from my book to help individuals and organizations accomplish important goals.

While I am not delving into each component of the formula, I am going to provide an explanation of the steps I use to accomplish all of my personal and professional goals.

As you might have noticed, I have a passion for the word *GREAT*. With my military background, I also have a fondness for acronyms. Let's take a closer look at the acronym G.R.E.A.T. to illustrate the steps required.

**The 5 GREAT Steps to Accomplishing Goals:**

| | | |
|---|---|---|
| **G**oals | – | Identify important **G**oals |
| **R**easons | – | Establish powerful **R**easons for accomplishing these goals |
| **E**xpectations | – | Set high **E**xpectations for yourself and your team |
| **A**ctions | – | Take all of the **A**ctions necessary |
| **T**racking | – | Intensely **T**rack your results |

To increase your success in accomplishing important goals for your organization, combine these five steps with the two other elements of *The GOAL Formula*: time and people. When you concentrate your efforts in a well–defined block of time, and also enlist the support of others, you will set and accomplish important short–term and long–term goals, increase your results, and experience new levels of success.

For more information on *The GOAL Formula*, visit my website: www.thinkgreat90.com

Identifying and accomplishing important goals is an educational process for leaders, helping them to realize what is necessary for the growth of their organization. Most businesses only need a carburetor adjustment for their engines, not a major overhaul. Leaders who make minor modifications will make major impacts with their important goals.

By linking together the six types of goals, ensuring that these goals have a positive impact, and by taking the necessary steps to accomplishing goals, you will not only realize your goals, but you will experience a dramatic enhancement in perceptions.

# PART II

## ELEVATE PRIORITIES

# PART II

## ELEVATE PRIORITIES

Focus "ON" Your Organization.

Is it possible for an object to move up and down at the same time? If you are a leader who has not learned how to effectively elevate priorities within your organization, you might often experience this phenomenon, which defies all laws of physics as well as the essence of leadership. Perhaps you have enjoyed the overwhelmingly positive feelings of rising up as a leader, while simultaneously experiencing that downward, sinking feeling of having too much on your plate.

As a coach, my primary audience members are leaders with full plates and unforgiving time constraints. Whether I train them one-on-one, as part of a team, or in front of hundreds at a workshop, they have all experienced the feeling of rising and falling at the same time.

When a leader fails to prioritize their leadership responsibilities, the key elements to growing their organization, they will experience high levels of frustration, stress, and disappointment. One of the greatest hazards faced by leaders is being pulled in too many directions. Your leadership position should not be a dumping ground of unaccomplished projects, but rather a fine-tuned factory of growth-oriented priorities.

From the moment you accept the position of leadership, every task, big and small, seems to become a hot rush, with the lion's share of the work resting on your shoulders. Projects that had been put on the back burner, miraculously find their way onto your desk as urgent, "Stop everything you're doing" emergencies.

Within three months of working at the post-production company in the entertainment industry, I earned my first leadership position. No sooner had my title changed when everything became a high-level mission.

Shift schedules, supplies, new hires, expenses, marketing, sales, etc. The list could go on and on, and it often does for most leaders. But I quickly learned that if everything is perceived as a "priority," then nothing is a true priority, and very little will be achieved.

## CREATE A SENSE OF URGENCY

Every organization is unique, consisting of vastly different goals for their overall strategic plan. Leaders must create a sense of urgency in order to elevate the priorities necessary for successful growth. While every action, task, and function performed within your organization should be important, and serve a specific purpose, not everything is a priority.

So how do you identify what is a priority and what is not? I use three simple words to help make the distinction between the negative, important, and priority elements within an organization: Out, In, and On.

OUT    – Negative actions that weaken your organization

IN    – Important tasks that operate your organization

ON    – Priority objectives that grow your organization

Successful leaders must be able to identify each of these elements, and also have a plan to remove, improve, or elevate each. While it might seem like common sense, far too many leaders fail to remove the "out-of-the-business" actions that do significant damage to their organization, and also to their reputation as a leader.

- "Out" actions can range from derogatory discussions among your staff about other team members, leaders, and departments to unnecessary, time-consuming steps in your workflow.

- "Out" actions are a result of weak leadership and a lackluster culture, resulting in a tremendous amount of wasted time, and a deep-seated resentment throughout the entire organization.

- These actions make it difficult to effectively lead your people and virtually impossible to grow your organization. Like a virus, negative actions will continue to grow unless they are properly treated

One of the first priorities of a leader is to identify and remove any "out" actions from your organization. As you enhance perceptions by clearly defining leadership, developing a unifying culture, and identifying important goals, you will find that many, who have mastered the "out" actions, will start to leave your team. As you elevate priorities, you will encourage and influence others to turn their attention to the "in" and "on" elements necessary for stability and growth.

While most leaders would quickly agree that their efforts should focus "on" the business, rather than "in" the business, they struggle to clearly articulate the difference between the two concepts.

- "In" activities are vitally important, helping to support your organization's goals.

- "On" activities move you closer to the important identified goals; those that help to develop a unifying culture and enhance perceptions.

Everything you do as a leader makes powerful connections, as long as you continue to link up the "on" objectives necessary for success. Leaders must strive to transfer their efforts from "in" the business to "on" the business.

For most of the leaders I have surveyed, the unfortunate ratio of "in" vs. "on" typically starts at about 90 percent "in" vs. 10 percent "on." When a leader can only allocate 10 percent of his or her time to the priorities necessary for growth, what results can be expected?

## HITTING THE TARGET

To elevate your priorities, which will help to stop the sinking feeling most leaders experience, let's take a closer look at "in" vs. "on." It is critical to make the distinction between these two elements, and to do so, let's go back to 1987, when I was a raw recruit in Marine Corps boot camp.

Sporting freshly shaved heads and wearing brand new camouflage uniforms, Platoon 1095 marched to the armory in our all-leather combat boots, which were still not broken in. The excitement of being issued our M-16A2 Assault Rifles was more than enough to help block out the pain from the fresh blisters on our feet.

Being issued our weapons was one thing, but mastering them would bring each recruit one step closer to our life-changing goal: earning the title of U.S. Marine. Because every Marine is a rifleman, regardless of what our job specialty was, this day had high level of intensity. We were enthusiastic and nervous at the same time. Have you ever felt like that?

From the moment my hands grasped my rifle, I began to understand the difference between important tasks and priority objectives. Having a much deeper understanding of both, our drill instructors created a sense of urgency for each. After hours of classroom training, endlessly practicing our breathing and aiming techniques, and repetitively firing hundreds of live rounds on the rifle range, we mastered every aspect about "how" our rifles worked.

We possessed an extensive knowledge about the important tasks (in) that we needed to operate our weapon. In less than a minute, we could disassemble and reassemble it, clean it to the point of looking like it had just come off of the assembly line, and we could march in perfect unison with it as if it were an extension of our own bodies. For a Marine, these are certainly important tasks.

But our priority objective (on) with this weapon was to fire it accurately in combat. To elevate this priority, our drill instructors used three distinct techniques.

1. They set high expectations for our performance.
2. They delegated specific portions of our rifle training to our Primary Marksmanship Instructors (PMIs).
3. They held us accountable, tracking every shot we fired.

Our drill instructors taught us more than just "how" to accurately hit a target from 500 yards away. They taught us "why" we needed to become proficient with our weapons. In a combat situation, our rifles could mean the difference between making it home from deployment, or having a flag sent home to be presented to your family. It could mean the difference between saving the Marines to your left and right, or watching them die.

Our drill instructors did much more than place a rifle in our hands, they taught us how to elevate priorities. With a sense of urgency, they instilled in us the difference between "in" and "on" by teaching us "how" to operate our weapons and "why" we needed to master them. To better understand the difference between "in" and "on" actions in your organization, let's take a quick look at a comparison between the two elements:

| IN Actions | ON Actions |
|---|---|
| Important | Priority |
| How? | Why? |
| Implement | Improve |
| Effective | Efficient |
| Short-term | Long-term |
| Train | Develop |
| Prepare | Plan |
| Tactical | Strategic |
| Recruit | Retain |
| Contact | Sell |
| Buy | Invest |
| Decrease Expenses | Increase Profitability |

While this list could easily be extended, it will give you a good idea of how to categorize all of the elements in your organization.

**Leadership Link** Make the distinction between the "in" and "on" actions in your organization, and increase the focus on important tasks, while simultaneously elevating high-priority objectives.

The tasks associated with operating our rifles were important. But focusing on our accuracy was a top priority. While it is probably safe to say that the environment your team works in is not life-threatening, even though some might act like it is, creating a sense of urgency will help you to be more effective at all of the "in" and "on" elements providing stability and growth.

I have found most leaders have over 80 percent of their time wasted because they are caught up with activities dedicated to working "in" their organization, or worse yet "out" of their organization. One of your goals will be to dedicate most of your time to the "on" actions necessary for growth.

As you eliminate the "out" actions and delegate (Chapter 5) the "in" actions, you will position yourself to focus the majority of your time "on" your priority objectives.

To elevate priorities:

1. Raise Expectations
2. Delegate with a Purpose
3. Increase Accountability

# Chapter 4

## Raise Expectations

Don't Set Low Expectations... You Might Hit Them.

Stepping off the bus at the Recruit Depot was a life-changing experience. Boot camp did not begin with a warm, fuzzy welcome from the Marine Corps. It erupted with yelling, shouting – and an insurmountable amount of confusion. To be clear, the yelling and shouting was the greeting we received from our drill instructors. The confusion was our reaction to this new environment and the Marines who controlled it.

Within in the first minute, we were formed up as a platoon. We stood at attention on the yellow footprints painted on the ground, positioned perfectly at a 45-degree angle. As we stood motionless, drill instructors swarmed around us and continued to bark commands, up close and personal, right in our faces.

There was no doubt boot camp would be physically and mentally challenging. As one of the drill instructors stepped up on a platform to address us, this became even more evident. With no uncertainty, he made it clear that not everyone of us would earn the title of U.S. Marine. Although we did not know the exact details of the training we would receive over the next 90 days, one thing was made crystal clear: their expectations.

Our drill instructors thoroughly communicated the message that the expectations on our performance were set high; Marine Corps high. Expectations were raised on our physical fitness, our appearance, and our communication. There were also expectations on everything from firing our weapons, spit-shining our boots, and Marine Corps leadership. By fully understanding the high expectations placed upon us, we were more focused on all of our actions.

How focused is your team on their actions?

## *ELIMINATE CONFUSION*

When is good not good enough? When great is achievable. But when leaders fail to clarify what is expected, they cannot "expect" to achieve high levels of success. Many leaders assume everyone knows what is expected of them, rather than ensuring that high expectations have been set and communicated throughout their organization.

Your team members are not mind readers. Putting them in a position to guess at what your expectations for them are is a guarantee for sub-par performance. Clearly articulating and documenting your expectations will increase performance, which will result in higher morale and results.

Throughout the twelve weeks of basic training, our drill instructors laid out their expectations, with great clarity, before assigning us our tasks. The recruits of Platoon 1095 knew exactly what was expected of them, and by graduation day, our drill instructors had successfully transformed a few, proud recruits into U.S. Marines.

What could you do in twelve weeks, if you properly raise expectations?

Most organizations have a significant gap between what the leader expects and what the leader experiences. This gap produces feelings of frustration and discouragement, not only for the leader, but for the team members as well. I have listened to leaders express, in great detail, their annoyance at the lack of their team members' performance. But I have also listened to team members express, in great detail, their annoyance at the lack of clear expectations set by their leaders.

This "expectation" gap will also create confusion and unwanted side effects. Wasted time, poor results, and low morale are only the beginning symptoms of this dilemma. Clearly articulating your expectations might seem like stating the obvious. But you owe it to yourself and to your team members to fill this gap with high expectations, leaving nothing to chance.

When you fail to set high expectations, you leave room for assumption, doubt, and misunderstanding. You probably noticed I re-emphasized the word high. While many leaders fail to set any expectations, others allow low expectations to infect their environment. Would you rather have your team meet high expectations or low expectations? The choice is yours. But so is the responsibility of raising those expectations.

I have found many leaders set low expectations because they have a fear of adding stress to their team. If high expectations create stress in a member of your team, you should analyze why that person is in your organization. Low expectations rarely shield anyone from stress. The same team member who feels threatened by high expectations is usually the same person who fails to live up to low expectations. Setting low expectations impacts your organizations in three ways

**The Impact of Low Expectations**:
1.  Protects low performers from higher performance
2.  Offends team members with high-performance potential
3.  Establishes you as a low-expectation leader

When leaders convey high expectations to their teams, they create a stronger belief level in their team members' perceptions of their own abilities, the focus of their leaders, and the upward mobility of their organization. If you do not have a strong belief in the abilities of your team, how can they?

In addition, leaders who raise expectations believe in themselves, their role as a leader, and their abilities to guide their teams and achieve results. If you do not believe in yourself, why would your team follow you? The answer is simple. They will not follow you or support you.

Many leaders make a crucial mistake when setting expectations. They only set them for their staff, leaving themselves out of the scenario. For everything, there is a starting point, and for raising expectations, it all begins with the leader.

## THE PRINCIPLES OF LEADERSHIP

As a do-it-first, lead-by-example leader, begin by setting high expectations for yourself in your role as a leader. Before you identify what you need to delegate to your team, and how to increase their accountability, clearly articulate what you are responsible for, and what your team can expect from your leadership.

To help enhance perceptions, by clearly defining leadership, we took a closer look at the 14 Leadership Traits of the U.S. Marine Corps. (Chapter 1). These traits have helped to provide the framework for the high levels of leadership that have been synonymous with the Marines since 1775.

Marines are also taught about eleven leadership principles that help to raise expectations of all Marine leaders. As you elevate priorities, adopt these principles, and they will help guide your actions with yourself and your team, providing a clear example of what is expected of a leader in your organization. Once your team understands what they can expect from you, they will deliver on what is expected of them.

Although you will not be marching your troops into life-threatening situations, you do have the ability to lead them into life-changing opportunities by raising expectations with unwavering conviction. Here's a closer look at the leadership principles of the Marine Corps, and how you can translate them into the high expectations needed to improve your performance as a leader.

### 11 Leadership Principles of the U.S. Marine Corps:

1. **Be Technically and Tactically Proficient** – Maintain a high level of competence in your job skills and leadership skills. Your proficiency will earn the respect of your team as you help them to problem solve, with excellent results. If you cannot understand their job, at the highest levels of excellence, how can you lead them to achieve greater results?

2. **Know Yourself and Seek Self Improvement** – Constantly evaluate your strengths and weaknesses. Improve your weaknesses and utilize

your strengths to gain an accurate understanding of yourself, and a keen-knowledge of determining the best way to deal with any given situation.

3. **Know Your Marines and Look Out for Their Welfare** – Get to know your team – personally and professionally. This is one of the most important, but overlooked principles. Know your team and how they react to different situations. Know them well enough to cast them in the right positions, for their personal growth, and the growth of your organization.

4. **Keep Your Marines Informed** – Providing information can inspire initiative. Informed team members perform better and, if knowledgeable of the situation, can carry on without your direct supervision. Too many leaders fail to keep their team members in the loop, undermining their own efforts. Communicate clearly and often.

5. **Set the Example** – Set the standards for your team by personal example. Your staff will observe your appearance, attitude, and performance. With high personal standards, you can expect the same of your team.

6. **Ensure the Task is Understood, Supervised, and Accomplished** – Before you can expect your team to perform, they need to know what is expected of them. Communicate your instructions in a clear, concise manner, and allow your team a chance to ask questions. Check progress periodically to confirm the assigned task is properly accomplished. *Delegate with a Purpose*, which we will cover in greater detail in Chapter 5.

7. **Train Your Marines as a Team** – Train your team with a purpose, and emphasize the essential elements of teamwork. Teach your staff to train, communicate, and operate as a team. Be sure all team members know their positions and responsibilities within the team framework.

8. **Make Sound and Timely Decisions** – Much can be lost when leaders hesitate to make decisions, especially in time-sensitive settings. Improving your internal workflow and raising expectations will allow you to con-

fidently and rapidly assess a situation and make a sound decision. There is no room for reluctance when making important decisions.

**9.  Develop a Sense of Responsibility in Your Subordinates** – Delegating important tasks promotes mutual confidence and respect between leaders and team members. Delegating decision-making is the ultimate form of trust and will show your team that you are interested in their personal growth by giving them the opportunity for professional development.

**10. Employ Your Unit in Accordance with its Capabilities** – Successful completion of a task depends upon how well you know your team's capabilities. Seek out challenging tasks for your staff, but be sure they are prepared for and have the ability to successfully complete the assignment. Train your team with a purpose.

**11. Seek Responsibility and Take Responsibility for Your Actions** – Actively seek out challenging assignments for your own professional development and take the responsibility for your actions. You are also responsible for all your team does or fails to do. Be willing to accept justified and constructive criticism. Team members respect leaders who correct their mistakes immediately.

These leadership principles are an essential tool for self-evaluation. By raising expectations for yourself, and seeking constant self-improvement, you can now rightfully set high expectations for your team. As you communicate what is expected of them you must properly transition tasks and authority to your team. To do so, it is imperative you delegate with a purpose.

# CHAPTER 5

## DELEGATE WITH A PURPOSE

*Properly Unload Your Plate.*

If you want something done right, do it yourself. How many times have you heard leaders utter this self-defeating statement? They say it to convey the inadequacies of others, but what it ultimately highlights is their short-comings as a leader; their inability to delegate. Leaders who believe they are the only ones capable of doing things right, are incapable of elevating the priorities necessary for growth in their organizations.

When I accepted an entry-level position at the post-production company, I started my first day with the highest expectations for my personal performance. While my position might have been at the bottom of the corporate ladder, my focus was at the top. I quickly mastered the duties and responsibilities of my job description, but I hungered for more.

Before I was in a position to delegate tasks, I requested that more were delegated to me. As I assumed responsibility for additional "in" tasks, my leaders could focus more of their attention "on" the priority objectives for the company. Mastering each of my new tasks, I began to help others to become more proficient at their duties. Constantly requesting and mastering the extra assignments delegated to me, resulted in three promotions in eighteen months.

My third promotion was to the position of vice president, and all of the leaders in the company now reported directly to me. I reported directly to the owner, and we were well on our way to increasing annual sales by over 300 percent. The art of delegation became one of the most critical disciplines I would embrace as I grew the company, and myself as a leader.

Each promotion presented new opportunities, but also introduced new challenges. My constantly changing job descriptions caused me to hand off more and more of my duties to my team. This was not something I took lightly. I knew the tasks I was transitioning to others still played a vital role in supporting the goals of the company, so I made the decision to delegate with a purpose.

## WHY LEADERS FAIL TO GROW

Tying your children's shoes makes sense when they are three years old. Tying their shoes when they are twenty-three years old, not so much. But it does speak volumes about your parenting skills, or more importantly, your lack of them. When leaders fail to properly transition important duties to their team members, it represents their own leadership limitations.

Far too many leaders are still doing the basic tasks they should have properly delegated to their team members long ago. Most leaders have a significant disconnect when it comes to delegation. Some transition responsibilities they should do themselves, while others fail to transition the duties their team members should be doing.

Delegating the important "in" tasks, necessary for effectively operating your organization, must be done with the highest levels of professionalism. While most leaders acknowledge the importance of delegating important tasks, they often leave out a critical component.

Properly delegating the task of tying shoes to your child is important, but delegating the decision-making ability of choosing the right shoes is more important. When a foot of snow is on the ground, tying a pair of sneakers is not as important as selecting the proper pair of snowshoes.

When you fail to delegate decision-making, in addition to the tasks, you might cause team members to reach an impasse and require far more of your time than you anticipated. When team members ask for additional information to complete a task, it is not uncommon to hear a leader mumble, "If I want something done right, I'll do it myself."

Here are two things you can do right, and should do yourself. When transitioning your duties to others, remember to delegate these two critical elements needed for success.

**Elements of Delegation**:

1. Delegate tasks

2. Delegate decision-making

Every leader will agree that delegation is necessary and will free up more time to focus on priority objectives, but most leaders experience little success when they attempt to transition duties to others. Delegating usually turns into nothing more than placing tasks onto someone else's plate, while the leader continues to maintain the decision-making abilities that would allow team members to take initiative and accomplish the task successfully.

In order to focus the majority of your efforts "on" priority objectives that will enhance your organization, leaders must accomplish many things through the efforts of others. The effective use of time, resources, and people will allow the leader, the team, and the company to grow simultaneously.

Leaders prohibit growth within their organizations by not properly delegating tasks and decision-making to their team members. With so much riding on the successful delegation of important tasks, you cannot afford to leave anything to chance.

## DELEGATE WITH A PURPOSE

One of the most common leadership topics I am requested to train on is delegation. Focused on achieving greater results, many leaders become frustrated at their inability to relinquish even the most basic tasks. Their desire to ensure that everything is completed correctly, matched with their ineffectiveness as a delegator, results in the perception that they are "control freaks" or "micro-managers."

With important tasks piling up on their plates, most leaders are often too busy handling the "in" items to be able to focus "on" the items necessary for growth. When I share the benefits of delegation with leaders, I am always met with nods of approval. To transform the delegation disconnect, into a leadership connection, I introduce a new delegation system.

As the vice president of a corporation that was experiencing exponential growth, delegation was my key to success. It was also the key to our high-level results. In order to delegate all of the tasks and decision-making necessary, I developed a process that would leave nothing to chance.

I found that delegation worked best when it was applied with detailed orchestration and direct supervision. To delegate with a purpose, always focus on the O.D.S. principle for success.

## Delegate with a Purpose – O.D.S.:

1. **O**rchestrate
2. **D**elegate
3. **S**upervise

With each delegated task, begin with a greater purpose; a reason for delegating. Identify why each item, every task, is important and how it supports the goals of your organization. When you convey the purpose to your team, you will develop a deeper buy-in from them.

Everything we did in the Marine Corps, even the tasks we despised, such as qualifying in the gas chamber, served a greater purpose. Our first encounter with the gas chamber occurred in boot camp. Each recruit spent approximately 3-5 minutes, perhaps the longest 3-5 minutes of our lives, in a chamber filled with chlorobenzylidene malononitrile, commonly referred to as CS Gas.

Typically used as a riot control agent, we were trained how to properly wear our masks in this environment. But the true test came when we were ordered to remove our masks. As the gas swirled around our faces, we held our breath and kept our eyes tightly closed. As we were instructed to "don and clear," we quickly placed our masks back on, covered our filters, and exhaled to blow any gas out of our masks.

We slowly opened our eyes and cautiously inhaled a small breath of air. Success! There was no air in our masks. Unfortunately, that was only the first part of being qualified. The next step was not as pleasant. We needed to experience the gas, without our masks.

One by one, we stepped up to our drill instructors. We were ordered to remove our masks and open our eyes. Holding my breath, I opened my eyes and they quickly felt the searing sting of the gas. To assist me in taking a breath, I was instructed to recite my general orders. I made it to number three when my lungs begged for air. I will never forget that moment.

My eyes were pouring tears from the unbearable burning sensation, and my lungs immediately shut down as they filled with gas. I could no longer breathe and it felt like I was dying. As I hurried out of the tent and into fresh air, I realized the greater purpose of this task – to stay alive. Learning how to operate in a hostile environment was critical, and our drill instructors had a deep level of buy-in from every member of Platoon 1095.

In addition to conveying the *purpose* of our assignment, our drill instructors *orchestrated* every variable involved with this task. They *delegated* the actions to us, complete with the training necessary for success. Leaving nothing to chance, they *supervised* our efforts and provided their guidance throughout the entire process.

When you delegate with a purpose, you are making a significant investment. It might seem like delegation will initially slow you down, but in the long run, it will increase productivity exponentially and allow you to further elevate priorities.

1. **Orchestrate** – consider all of the possible variables in any given assignment you are delegating. If something can go wrong, it probably will. This is precisely why you need to identify any decision-making duties that will support the completion of the task.

Orchestration is more than coordination. It is the creation of the blueprints for success, combining three crucial steps.

**To Orchestrate**: Plan – Train – Allocate

Having a clear plan for the successful completion of each task, will allow you to communicate the high expectations you have for its completion. Your plan must include the procedures, the variables, and the solutions needed for positive results.

As you develop the details of your plan, factor in any necessary training needed, prior to delegating the task. While some leaders have every detail coordinated, they fail to train the team member responsible for the task, setting the person up for failure from the outset.

Processes that seem simple and straightforward to the leader might not be so easy for someone who has never encountered them before. Too many leaders assign tasks to people who are not properly trained, and this ultimately results in frustration and resentment for everyone.

Be patient and realize that training also requires you to listen to their questions and concerns. It should go without saying that the orchestration phase is the best time to hear their thoughts. Unfortunately, many leaders wait until the task has already been delegated. You should always anticipate questions. Deciding which phase this happen in is up to you.

Training is a long-term investment in your delegation system. Be mindful that the time spent in the training process will significantly minimize the time spent correcting mistakes.

The last component of the orchestration phase is to allocate all of the resources required to complete the task. Forms and documents, passwords, and equipment need to be readily available to allow timelines to be met. If you do not orchestrate effectively, you will pay the price later.

2.   **Delegate** – detailed orchestration makes the delegation phase simple and effective. Having invested the necessary time in planning, training, and allocating resources, your communication will be clear, concise, and well-received by everyone involved in the assignment. The negative perception of "dumping" projects will soon transform into a results-oriented transition of tasks and decision-making.

During this phase, provide any additional clarification about the task and the decision-making needed, and also allow your team members the opportunity to ask any additional questions. To boost the confidence of your staff, reemphasize the support they can expect from you and anyone else involved with this task.

Offering the proper support is the key to not becoming the dreaded "micro-manager." I have always found it beneficial to articulate how I successfully accomplished the task, while leaving room for the individual to do it in ways that work best for them. Focus more on the results and less on the formality of the procedure. When you treat someone like a person who is capable of taking initiative, they will typically be more inclined to take it.

3. **Supervise** – now that you have delegated the task you so diligently orchestrated, you will need to regularly connect with your team about their progress. Supervising is about course-correcting. Set up meetings, as needed, to discuss strengths and weaknesses. Allow your team to communicate their challenges, and offer constructive feedback for their development. This is the time to help them to problem-solve. Guiding them through their failures will build trust and confidence.

Each phase should require less of your time, but more of your direct input. Delegating with a purpose takes an investment on your part, but pays you back in more ways than you can ever calculate. Now that you have learned how to delegate with a purpose, it is time to further elevate priorities as you *Increase Accountability.*

# CHAPTER 6

## INCREASE ACCOUNTABILITY

Changing Behaviors is Better Than Punishing Performance.

"When am I going to get those reports?"

"When is that thing going to be finished?"

"Who dropped the ball on that order?"

"Who's responsible for that?"

Does any of this sound familiar? In most organizations, leaders ask these types of questions more than they should, often receiving the same answer, "I don't know, it's not my job!"

Without a doubt, it is important to know who is responsible. But an even-more crucial question should be, "How can we improve?" Without the proper accountability in place, leaders and team members will encounter more frustration and less trust. When the workplace lacks accountability it misses out on opportunities for growth, most of which are in plain sight.

As you *Set High Expectations* and *Delegate with a Purpose*, you must also *Increase Accountability*. Raising the bar on personal responsibility throughout your organization, by providing a standard expectation of accountability everyone clearly understands, will allow you to further *Elevate Priorities*. Accountability removes the fog clouding your team's vision.

Failure to implement accountability will result in the blame game. Tactical solutions will be replaced by finger pointing, creating a negative impact on you, your team, and your customers. Without accountability, the path to sustainable growth is nearly invisible. Accountability will help your organization to increase productivity and team morale, while simultaneously improving customer satisfaction. While it will bring great results –

many leaders struggle with the implementation and maintenance of this powerful tactic.

## THE OBSTACLES OF ACCOUNTABILITY

With the hopes of stellar performance, leaders often dream about the results they will see as their team members voluntarily and enthusiastically assume high levels of personal responsibility. Think about it for a moment – commitments upheld, rules being followed, tough decisions being resolved, sales numbers up, and expenses down.

This dream scenario is usually short-lived. Once awake, the obstacles of accountability create stress and frustration for leaders at all levels within an organization. Those who believe in the positive benefits of accountability often struggle to successfully implement it within their teams. Accountability is typically perceived with great pessimism by most employees, associating it with negativity, discipline, and punishment.

Unfortunately, these dismal perceptions are accurate, rooted deeply in the failures of other leaders. When a leader lacks the dedication and commitment necessary to eliminate the three obstacles of accountability, their organization suffers. Standards begin to slip and people fail to perform up to their true potential.

**3 Obstacles of Accountability**:

1. Lack of Action

2. Focus on Poor Performance

3. Failure to Recognize Achievement

1. **Lack of Action** – accountability is not taken seriously because it typically receives more lip service than action. Most leaders use reports to show team members that they are aware of their efforts, but offer little-to-no constructive recommendations on how to improve their performance. Some leaders track too little, while others track too much. Regardless of

the quantity, a common frustration among team members is that nothing is done positively with the information collected.

Unacknowledged accountability is despised by everyone. When someone takes the time, puts in the effort, and uses resources to provide a leader with an accountability report, some form of action is expected. To do or say nothing about it results in discouragement. Ultimately, you will begin to receive the bare minimums of what you are requesting.

**Leadership Link** Only track something that you are prepared to take action on.

2.  **Focus on Poor Performance** – in most organizations, accountability is set in motion for the wrong reason – to fix a negative situation. "Too many people are late to work, so we'll track their attendance." "Sales are down, so let's track their contacting efforts." "Expenses are too high, so we need to track their spending." Leaders who step in only when something is wrong are perceived as the bearers of bad news, and team members become uneasy in their presence.

After a series of intense meetings, warnings, and write-ups, performance might briefly improve, causing the focus on accountability to decrease. As the performance begins to dip again, accountability is again raised. This negative cycle causes a temporary change in patterns, but not the permanent enhancements in behavior required to achieve greater results.

**Leadership Link** Use the power of tracking to end the cycles of poor performance.

3.  **Failure to Recognize Achievement** – leaders tend to focus their time and efforts on fixing the negative performance of their low-performing

team members, rather than recognizing the positive performance of their star players.

Over time, a lack of accountability will cause deep resentment in those who have provided outstanding performance. When more attention is dedicated to poor performance than top-tier achievement, these team members will seek organizations that embrace accountability and reward excellent performance.

Conversely, the organization lacking accountability struggle to attract top talent because those types of professionals need to be in an environment that values their positive attributes of accountability.

**Leadership Link**   Begin to track the elements that will provide opportunities for recognition.

As you eliminate the 3 Obstacles of Accountability, you will deliver more recognition for high performance, and dedicate less time reprimanding low performance. Accountability is much more than receiving a spread sheet with some numbers. It is a plan for success – and for building a better organization.

## LEADERSHIP TOOLS

Leaders are builders. Successful leaders build team members, new leaders, and strong organizations. It is detrimental to your success to do it with the use of tools. Tools help to collapse time frames, allowing for greater precision, and ultimately producing greater results.

In Ethiopia, the earliest findings show that man learned the importance of creating and enhancing tools approximately 2.6 million years ago. Specialized stone tools, used for hammering, fighting, hunting and butchering animals, were not just stumbled upon, they were manufactured. They were designed to support an important goal: survival.

Even chimpanzees understand the benefit of using basic tools to hunt their prey and forage for ants. But it is the extent to which humans have developed and utilized tools that makes it one of the greatest factors that separates us from animals. What separates you from other leaders? What tools are you using to improve the results of your team, your results as a leader, and the results of your organization?

The failure of accountability can be directly linked to the ineffective use, or complete disregard, of the leadership tools necessary to raise the bar on performance and achieve greater results. After all, isn't that what accountability should be focused on: performance and results? Using the following leadership tools, will allow you to create a system for increasing accountability.

**Leadership Tools for Increasing Accountability**:

1. Goals
2. Organizational Chart
3. Job Descriptions
4. Workflow
5. Evaluations

Before we take a closer look at the vital importance of each tool, understand that most of the leaders who I encounter have tried, unsuccessfully, to build their team and their organization without using leadership tools. They strive for greater results, but leave the required tools untouched in their toolboxes.

When I ask for the current version of these tools, I typically get a response such as, "Um... hold on for a second... you know, actually we're still updating them." Yes, it is difficult to use a hammer if is still being manufactured.

Most organizations have some version of these tools, but merely check them off of a list as "completed." When leaders fail to take them out of their toolbox and use them for their true purpose, they fail to effectively increase accountability. Separate yourself from other leaders by strengthening, implementing, and utilizing these powerful tools.

1. **Goals** – the important goals you identified in Chapter 3 were never meant to be tucked away. These goals are the driving force for accountability, and provide clarity and certainty. Everything your organization does should support the accomplishment of these goals.

Important goals magnify the passion needed to create high levels of accountability, while providing the team with direction and clarity. Increasing accountability is not about providing the leader with information, it is about analyzing key data and course-correcting to ensure that the goals are not only met, but exceeded.

Regularly discuss the important goals of your organization, especially as it relates to all forms of accountability.

2. **Organizational Chart** – just as a sports coach draws the "X's" and "O's" on a play chart, leaders must position their team members for the big win. Organizational charts are rarely visible in most organizations, but they are the first link to accomplish the important goals.

More than assigning a name to a job, your organizational chart identifies the positions and people necessary to support the accomplishment of the goals. Every position should serve a purpose, and every person should play an important role.

Accountability will help to identify the positions needed, and those no longer required. As your organizational chart evolves to meet the needs of your goals, it will provide a snapshot of the current and future team required for success.

In just one year, the organizational chart that I created, changed three times; eliminating, adding, and enhancing the positions necessary to support our current and future growth.

3. **Job Descriptions** – people struggle to be accountable when the expectations from their leaders are not clearly defined and written down.

When job descriptions are used, many leaders hand them out with a stack of other documents to be reviewed by the team member, not used as a tool to outline the high expectations for their performance.

It is hard to hold anyone accountable when there is ambiguity with their role. This leads to confusion and a lack of initiative. Job descriptions are powerful tools for accountability, and open up the line of communication with everyone. Each word on that form should have a definitive purpose.

When creating job descriptions, include the following:

- Position Overview – how this role supports the goals
- Essential Duties – what each team member is responsible for
- Requirements – the skills required for success
- Signatures – both the team member and the leader sign the form

By having both the leader and the team member sign the document, each person will be responsible for ensuring that the team member is 100 percent proficient at the required elements for the position. Job descriptions should constantly be reviewed as they highlight key areas of training needed to get that person fully qualified to perform those duties.

4. **Workflow** – every organization has specific policies, procedures, and best practices for "how" things need to be done properly. If they do not, they need them. Workflow is the process of enhancing efficiencies and eliminating mistakes. Workflow tells those "who" are responsible for doing something, "how" to do it.

Whether your team processes orders, ships materials, or submits forms internally, a detailed workflow will allow the work to transition from start to finish, with the least amount of resistance. Once designed, workflow can be easily modified to accommodate new products, services, regulations, etc.

In the media business, with the support of my leadership team, we invested our time and resources to create a workflow system that helped reduce our out-going error ratio from 15% to .35%. Yes, almost one-third of one percent. Our workflow increased the number of people checking the status of each order, and it significantly decreased our error ratio.

Our improvements resulted in less mistakes and more satisfied customers. Our team could fulfill the expectations in their job descriptions and our customers could count on us for outstanding results. Develop a workflow that will allow everyone to do their jobs with the highest possibility for success. For many leaders, the perfect workflow exists in their heads. Taking the time necessary to show the proper protocols to your team will eliminate the, "If I want something done right ..." dialogue.

5.  **Evaluations** – too many leaders miss out on the amazing opportunities they have to provide guidance, coaching, and positive course-correcting. They neglect to set regular performance evaluations, leaving the personal and professional development of their team members to their own vices. How well do you think that works?

Leaders often mistake intent for performance, not realizing that their team members have a strong desire for improvement. By having solid job descriptions, as well as an effective workflow system, you are armed to provide the necessary feedback for success. As you discuss the duties and responsibilities you both have signed off on, you will open up honest dialogue for improvement. You might also hear powerful suggestions on how to make things even better.

Accountability allows leaders to gain valuable insight and discover new opportunities for growth. It also identifies the necessary positions and the team members needed to get the job done. Accountability not only allows you to *Elevate Priorities*, but it helps to strengthen your ability to *Empower People*.

**Leadership Link**    Conduct evaluations regularly and search for areas of improvement and opportunities to recognize great performance.

# PART III

## EMPOWER PEOPLE

# Part III

## Empower People

Move from Readiness to Preparation.

I let out a huge sigh of relief as I clicked "Save," signaling that the final touches on our infrastructure had been completed. All of our t's were crossed and our i's were dotted. It was a major undertaking, but overhauling our policies and procedures helped us to outline everything our team needed in order to be ready for the high levels of growth we were projecting.

Our organizational chart depicted the necessary team structure, while our job descriptions detailed the duties and responsibilities of each employee. By improving our sales system and upgrading our operational workflow, we further increased our ability to succeed. Everyone knew what was expected and we were ready to pursue the important goals necessary to take our company to the next level. But one question lingered in the back of my mind. We might have been ready for growth, but would we be prepared for the challenges ahead of us?

I knew the dramatic difference between being ready – and being prepared. Flashing back to 1987, I remember the intense training I received as a young Marine. Attached to every task and objective were the highest levels of excellence. Being proficient in my job duties as an air traffic controller, and qualifying as a sharp shooter with my rifle, made me feel ready for anything. But the Marine Corps never settles on only being ready.

August 2, 1990 was the day before my 21st birthday. It was also the same day the world watched as Iraq invaded Kuwait. On that day, the United States prepared for war. As Operation Desert Storm drew closer, I remember my thoughts shifting from how ready I was; to how prepared was I? My service in the Corps had covered three years, but during peace time.

Everything changed on that day as we headed toward the rising conflict in the Middle East.

Our leaders ensured that we were ready for deployment by supplying us with all of the necessary gear. From head to toe, we carried nearly 80 pounds of equipment. Loaded with helmets, flak jackets, ammunition, and canteens, we strapped on our back packs, which were filled with the additional gear necessary for life in the field.

Our orders, the "policies and procedures" we would be following, were communicated to us in great detail. Every Marine clearly understood the mission. The objectives, that were necessary to accomplish our goals, were of the highest priority. We were ready. But in the brief time leading up to our deployment, our leaders ensured that we were also prepared.

Providing us with much more than supplies and orders, our leaders empowered us with the ability to take ownership of our situation; to take the initiative needed to succeed. On my 21st birthday, our training immediately commenced in the excruciating heat of the Yuma desert.

Wearing full combat gear, we marched through the sandy terrain, which resembled the harsh Saudi Arabian environment where we would soon be deployed. As we continued to move forward, under the unrelenting temperatures, our leaders presented us with challenges to sharpen our skills. They provided every opportunity possible to empower us, not all of which were pleasant.

Through the blistering heat, often breaking 115 degrees, gas canisters were launched in our direction, simulating a chemical attack by the enemy. Having our masks made us ready, but being able to effectively use them under extreme conditions and circumstances helped us to be prepared. But what if a fellow Marine was not able to put on his mask fast enough? We were empowered to think on our feet.

Each Marine was issued 2 PAM Chloride, a nerve agent treatment. Using auto-injector devices, we could effectively administer this life-saving chemical to ourselves, or a fellow Marine. Thrusting the injector into the outer thigh muscle, a powerful dose would be released from the needle and into the bloodstream.

As new challenges were introduced, the Marines in my unit faced them with the highest levels of professionalism and resolve. Our leaders empowered us with the ability to take the initiative necessary to employ fast-acting, life-saving decisions without having to wait for the order to do so. How does your team currently handle challenges? Are they handling them the way you desire?

While my father's poor health prevented me from being deployed, my unit was sent to Saudi Arabia to support Operation Desert Storm. The Marines in my platoon were not only ready for the difficult circumstances ahead, they were prepared for a successful campaign.

## EMPOWERING YOUR TEAM

The level of training I received in the Marine Corps showed me the difference between being ready and being prepared. It also emphasized the need for leaders to channel their energy on empowering people. As an executive corporate leader, focused on growth, my ability to empower people would become a determining factor in achieving greater results.

At the post-production company, I had enhanced perceptions and elevated priorities, but I knew our success would not be achieved if I failed to empower the people in our organization. I was determined to replace the old way of thinking with a new environment of innovation; one that allowed our employees to transform from "do-what-I-have-to-do" performers to "out-of-the-box" thinkers.

When leaders present new opportunities for growth to their teams, they are often met with, "Here's why we can't do it." To achieve sustainable upward momentum, leaders need empowered team members who choose the option, "Here's how we can do it."

Imagine walking into your office and being surrounded by a team of people who take ownership of their duties and responsibilities. Think about the benefits of having employees who focus their efforts on finding solutions and creating opportunities, rather than identifying problems and settling for average.

Most leaders would do anything possible to have a team of proactive, empowered people who can function as both a cohesive unit and succeed autonomously. But the problem is they do not do everything necessary to have a team like this. The leader is often the root of the problem, inadvertently creating a dismal mindset in their organization, rather than a culture of empowerment.

Leaders ignore empowerment because they do not truly understand it. It is not assigning a task to be completed; that is achieved by proper delegation. Empowerment is not providing instructions, nor is it leaving someone to their own devices. Neither is it micro-management.

Empowerment is about helping your team to achieve personal growth and autonomy. It is about presenting them with opportunities to think for themselves, and to make decisions confidently. When you empower people, you give them the authorization to take initiative, to be creative, and to become independent. When you empower people, you transform them from reactive to proactive. After all, doesn't every leader want a proactive team?

But if it were easy to empower people, every leader would do it. Leaders must ensure that their environment encourages employees to take initiative, rewarding them for taking action without being asked. This can be fostered by linking together three elements that allow an environment to thrive!

1. Communication
2. Cultivation
3. Collaboration

When the people are empowered, the environment promotes creativity. As team members take more initiative, they will find new solutions they might have missed had they adhered to rigid guidelines.

Leaders who recognize their people for their ideas, will instill a sense of pride and accomplishment, encouraging further initiative. Empowering your people will break them out of the traditional boss-employee mind-set, and will build trust, self-confidence, and achievement.

**Leadership Link**  When you empower people, you allow them to unleash their full potential, positioning your organization for new levels of success.

# CHAPTER 7

## COMMUNICATION

*Leaders Make an Impact.*

Learning to focus on enunciation and vocabulary, grammar and punctuation, we are taught an understanding of our language from our earliest days of school. But the skills needed to properly speak and write do not qualify us to lead people, much less empower them. To make the leadership connection with communication, more than an academic approach is necessary.

The communication styles of most leaders vary significantly.

- Some can be passive while others take a more aggressive approach.
- Some use elements of manipulation while others choose motivation.
- Leaders can be assertive, direct, and crystal-clear.
- They can also be vague, indirect, and misleading.

Regardless of their style, each leader sends a message every time they communicate. This message reaffirms their strength and weaknesses – their conviction to the greater purpose of the organization, and their ability to successfully guide their team to the desired destination. A leader's message must be a consistent, positive, reassurance about their intent.

To measure the effectiveness of a message being sent, leaders can rank their level of communication by using three categories. Identifying the type of communication used in your organization will allow you to make the adjustments necessary to transform it into a tool of empowerment.

**3 Levels of Communication**:

1. Poor

2. Basic

3. Dynamic

Leaders can typically trace organizational problems, issues, and challenges back to poor communication. When dialogue fails to deliver the appropriate message, companies experience significantly more damage than the initial mistakes caused only by misunderstandings.

Poor communication will erode a leader's ability to enhance perceptions, elevate priorities, and empower people. No matter how minor, the impact of poor communication can have long-term effects.

**The Impact of Poor Communication**:

1. Destroys morale

2. Minimizes effectiveness

3. Discourages innovation

4. Reduces efficiencies

5. Eliminates collaboration

Poor communication often occurs when leaders use it as a device to simply transition information from one person to the next. By failing to attach a distinct message to their dialogue, their ambiguity inadvertently leaves room for unintended interpretations of their comments.

Awareness of poor communication is the first step. The next step, toward the creation of an environment that fosters a high level of empowerment, is developing a mastery of basic communication skills.

## BASIC COMMUNICATION

I have yet to meet a leader who set out to be a poor communicator. Most leaders do not plan to fall short in this important arena. But when knowledge of basic communication skills is absent, only sub-par results can be achieved. Leaders who are reluctant to embrace basic communication skills, will magnify the barriers preventing their message from reaching their audience.

Both physical and psychological barriers can create a filtering effect and lessen the impact of a leader's message. Communication barriers such as stress, culture, noise, and perception can filter out important components of a leader's dialogue. Great communicators develop a keen external awareness of any obstacles to communication, and put forth great efforts to minimize their impact by maximizing their basic communication skills.

Involving much more than merely coordinating dialogue, leaders must ensure that their message is able to pass through any barrier existing between them and their audience. Effective communicators develop an understanding of the three elements of basic communication.

**The 3 Elements of Basic Communication**:

1. Words
2. Body language
3. Actions

**Words** – the invisible tools that have the ability to influence thoughts and behaviors. In addition to choosing the appropriate words to convey a message, leaders should pay particular attention to the tone of their voices. Certainty and conviction will be translated more by the inflections of the voice, than by the actual spoken words.

**Leadership Link**   Choose your words wisely and deliver them with passion.

**Body Language** – every gesture, from hand movements and eye contact, to facial expressions and body posture, signals the audience about the true nature of the leader's feelings. While people are listening to a leader speak, they are watching every move intently to develop a deeper understanding of the meaning behind the message.

**Leadership Link**   Be aware of your verbal and non-verbal communication.

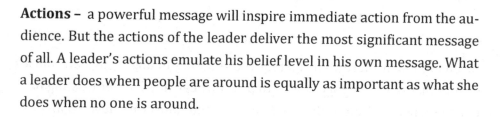

**Actions –** a powerful message will inspire immediate action from the audience. But the actions of the leader deliver the most significant message of all. A leader's actions emulate his belief level in his own message. What a leader does when people are around is equally as important as what she does when no one is around.

**Leadership Link**   One bad action will undermine a thousand great words.

## CORPS COMMUNICATION

You could hear a pin drop as the bus door swung open. Calculated and meticulous, a Marine Corps drill instructor (DI) stepped in, turned, and faced us. Still wearing our civilian clothes, we sat there in silence, but not for long. With an explosion of dynamic communication, and colorful words I cannot write in this book, the sergeant communicated that we needed to quickly exit that bus. Within seconds, each seat was empty.

Boot camp had officially begun. Over the next ninety days, the communication we experienced from our drill instructors was much more than barking orders, screaming instructions, and yelling at the top of their lungs. Yes, the DI's had a highly elevated volume of dialogue, but the purpose behind their communication was empowerment.

Everything our drill instructors did had a greater purpose. Their words, their body language, and their actions did more than just instruct us; they molded us. Marine leaders do not use communication merely to translate orders to the troops. They use it to empower their Marines during the most challenging situations.

Marine Corps legend, "Chesty" Puller, harnessed the power of dynamic communication. Lewis Puller, affectionately known to his men as "Chesty," because of his huge barrel-shaped chest, served our great nation for thirty-seven years. Starting out as an enlisted man, he worked his way up to the rank of a three-star general.

Lieutenant General Puller is synonymous with Marine Corps leadership. Among his numerous decorations, he was awarded five Navy Crosses, the Bronze Star, and the Purple Heart. He was a true master of communication and this became evident during some of the bloodiest battles of World War II and the Korean War.

Imagine for a moment that you are a young Marine in Chesty's command. You are in sub-zero temperatures at the Chosin Reservoir in Korea. Thousands of miles from home, you stand on enemy soil with your fellow Marines. You are vastly outnumbered, and the odds are that you will not survive through the day. How important would your leader's communication be to you at this moment in your life?

As legend has it, Chesty boldly assessed the dire situation for his Marines. "They are in front of us, behind us, and we are flanked on both sides by an enemy that outnumbers us 29 to 1." If you were one of the Marines in his ranks, this might not have been the dialogue you wanted to hear. But it was crystal clear.

With lives on the line, Chesty did not end his communication there. Moving beyond basic communication, he added seven words of dynamic communication as he finished addressing his Marines. "They can't get away from us now!" How powerful was that extra dialogue to the men of 1st Marine Regiment? It was life-changing. The Marines not only won the battle, but they destroyed seven enemy divisions in the process.

While the Marines lost 836 lives during this battle, the enemy suffered loses of nearly 35,000. Chesty's Marines looked to him for inspiration and motivation. But he delivered more than that by empowering them with every well-placed word. With dynamic communication, he changed their belief levels about their circumstances and empowered them to achieve more than they thought possible.

My devotion to this level of communication did not end when my tour of duty did. It has remained with me, and I have applied it to every aspect of my personal and professional life. Dynamic communication does not happen by chance, it happens by choice. Successful leaders do not empower people as a side effect of their words, their body language, and their actions. It is the driving purpose every time they communicate.

Is dynamic communication happening in your organization?

## IMPROVING COMMUNICATION

Training leaders on the importance of sending the right message, I typically encounter the universal response, "I need to improve my communication skills." Leaders absolutely need to focus on improving their dialogue, because everything they say and do is constantly under scrutiny; analyzed and interpreted by everyone receiving their message.

Required to speak in many settings, leaders communicate one-on-one, to teams, at meetings, and through various forms of correspondence. Improving basic communication skills is essential, and it starts by realizing communication is always a two-way process. It is never enough just to be heard; a leader must ensure that she has been understood.

Often times, many leaders look back on conversations and wish they had phrased things differently. The moment the words left their mouths, they knew they were not going to be interpreted as well as they had hoped. But hope is not a viable strategy when so much rides on developing dialogue that delivers a powerful message. To improve your communication skills, focus on three simple steps.

**The 3 Steps to Improving Basic Communication**:

1. Listening

2. Preparation

3. Delivery

**Listening** – leaders must pay particular attention to what people have to say. But they often mistake hearing for listening. Hearing is nothing more than registering the sounds entering your ears. Listening requires more; it requires focus.

Listening allows a leader to connect with the audience and understand their story, through their verbal and non-verbal signals. Listening allows a leader to anticipate the receiver's viewpoint and feelings, formulate a deeper message, and increase the chances of empowering people.

**Preparation** – leaders must plan their communication, especially when delivering a powerful message. Too many try to "wing-it" when they share important dialogue with their teams, and thus the results are often less than anticipated. Being prepared allows a leader to understand his audience, stay on target with key points, and achieve his outcome.

While some instances might not allow a leader to fully develop a plan for communication, a leader who focuses on improving basic communication skills will always feel more prepared to interact with people, turning impromptu situations into empowering exchanges.

**Delivery** – leaders must do more than speak. They need to make an impact. Everything has led to this moment; the moment of transferring a planned message to the audience. Rather than over-emphasizing problems, successful communicators deliver powerful solutions.

In addition to providing the necessary statistics to support the message, leaders who share relatable stories increase their connection to their audiences. Personal stories and passion resonate deeper than graphs and charts. Express meaning with conviction in your delivery and you will connect the importance of your message to the goals of the organization and the goals of your audience.

## DYNAMIC COMMUNICATION

As a professional speaker, personal coach, and corporate trainer, my ability to deliver a powerful message each time I communicate is paramount. My business depends on my capability to provide dynamic communication, giving empowering messages to people to achieve greater results. Of course, isn't that what every leader should be striving for when they communicate?

I think it is fair to say all organizations would benefit from leaders who placed an emphasis on high levels of communication. But understanding the need for empowering people and carrying it out are two different things. Even the leaders who see the value in dynamic communication are often ill-prepared to follow through with it.

The first step to developing dynamic communication is to view every interaction as the opportunity to make a significant impact in the life of the person with whom you are connecting. No matter how brief the dialogue, leaders must possess a desire to empower that person, team, or audience.

As I became more aware of the dynamic possibilities of my own communication, I looked for common denominators I could easily repeat, and achieve high levels of empowerment. I analyzed how my words, body language, and actions affected people and influenced them to reach for new heights.

I narrowed my style of dynamic communication to three main points. Not only could I intertwine these elements into virtually any conversation, and see results, but I could train other leaders how to do the same for their teams. Now, if I could create a way for them to remember these three points.

In the Marine Corps, we were required to remember many important things. Everything from understanding how our rifles operated to the function of our back-packs, had an acronym to help with memorization.

**Rifle: LMGAS** - **L**ightweight, **M**agazine-fed, **G**as-operated, **A**ir-cooled, **S**houlder-fired weapon

**Back Pack: ALICE** - **A**ll-purpose, **L**ight-weight, **I**ndividual **C**arrying **E**quipment

As seen in Chapter 1, I shared the acronym for remembering the 14 Leadership Traits of the Marine Corps - JJ DID TIE BUCKLE. It goes without saying that I would use an easy-to-remember acronym to keep dynamic communication on the forefront of a leader's thoughts and remind them to add these elements into their conversations.

**BEC - The Elements of Dynamic Communication**:

1. Believe
2. Encourage
3. Challenge

Believe in people, encourage them to grow, and challenge them to unleash their true potential. Most leaders communicate about what they find to be wrong, and people usually stop wanting to hear more from these leaders. To empower, when you search for what has been done right and build on it, people will start to look forward to hearing more from you.

**1. Believe** – leaders need to let people know they believe in them, and they matter. A leader's accomplishments and expertise have less of an impact than the expression of her sincere belief in an individual.

Expressing belief in someone is a powerful tool for a leader. It communicates trust, which is one of the strongest connections a leader can make with their team members. Belief validates people and helps them to draw on their own strengths to navigate through difficult circumstances.

A leader's belief in someone must be genuine and authentic; it cannot be faked. When leaders show a belief in others, it also communicates a belief in themselves. It shows people you possess a confidence and certainty about your own abilities.

To be successful, leaders must believe in the individuals on their teams, the team as a whole, their organization, and themselves.

**2. Encourage** – leaders who encourage people, help bring about significant changes in the lives of others. Encouragement provides people with the ability to make shifts. Encouragement gives people the power to change their behaviors, their results, and their destiny.

Most people feel overwhelmed and overworked. The challenges of life causes many to experience discouragement, which creates lackluster performance and poor attitudes. Leaders who encourage people to make the necessary changes to succeed, make them feel stronger, more energized, and more excited. When people are encouraged, they find the inner fortitude to make things happen; things that would have seemed impossible unless they were encouraged with dynamic communication.

Leaders who want to encourage people must invest the time to get to know them. Communicate with the purpose of gaining a deeper understanding of their challenges. Get to know co-workers as people, not just employees. You might be surprised at what you discover, as they begin to communicate suggestions for greater possibilities.

**3. Challenge** – leaders who challenge people, do much more than "dare" them to grow. They empower them to develop. Presenting the right challenge to someone can reiterate a strong belief in them, encourage them to make positive changes, and enable them to see their true potential. Empowering someone might actually allow him to exceed his potential.

To challenge someone, you must engage her in deeper levels of communication and search for the areas that mean the most to her. Actively seek areas where people have stalled, and where they have reached a plateau in their own growth. These are the areas where you can help them to overcome the obstacles in their own path to greatness.

Great leaders empower others with the solutions needed to overcome their obstacles, to grow, and to develop. Communication is one of the few components of leadership always in your control. You can provide dynamic communication that empowers everyone you encounter.

# Chapter 8

## Cultivation

*Train People to Know More. Cultivate People to Grow More.*

Teamwork! Let's say it again. Teamwork. This one word conjures up positive feelings of camaraderie and success, energy and excitement. Imagine what your organization would be like, if it were filled with driven, self-starting team players who all strive for excellence. The possibilities would be limitless. But that is not necessarily what occurs in most organizations.

Coaching, mentoring, and guiding powerful, dynamic teams is the aspiration of anyone who embraces his role as a leader. But instead, most leadership duties revolve around monitoring people who struggle to work together and who barely fulfill the minimum requirements of their job descriptions.

Teamwork is an integral part of an organization's success. Transforming a group of employees into a cohesive team requires much more than training. It requires a commitment to cultivating each member. Cultivation allows employees and leaders to band together, maximizing their efficiency and achieving common objectives. The benefits of teamwork are too important to take a casual approach.

**The Benefits of Teamwork:**

1. Synergy
2. Effectiveness
3. Resourcefulness

**1. Synergy** – the same fingers that can point the blame at others, can join together with the hands of other positive team members to create an unbreakable bond. A synergistic team achieves peak performance by understanding their roles, sharing the workload, and working together for the greater good of the organization.

**Effectiveness** – most people go to work. Effective teams excitedly show up to make an impact. They work together to increase each others performance, which eliminates wasted time and increases results.

**Resourcefulness** – members of dynamic teams present solutions, discovering new ways of doing things. Resourceful teams strive to see the process of each project through to completion.

How would it feel to lead a synergistic, effective, and resourceful team? It feels GREAT! But leaders who fail to create an environment of teamwork, have usually failed to put in the work required to properly develop a team of this level. Teamwork does not magically occur by appointing people to a roster. It is the result of cultivating the talent and untapped potential of each member.

Cultivating a team provides distinct advantages, not only to the members of the team, but also to anyone who encounters the team. How important is "cultivation" to a leader? Simply put, it means the difference between growing an organization, or allowing it to wither and die.

## FARMING FOR SUCCESS

Studies show that nearly 40 percent of employees are dissatisfied with their bosses, and over 70 percent feel disengaged at their current jobs. I have yet to meet a leader who set out to create feelings of dissatisfaction and disengagement among his team members. But these are the unfortunate results when leaders do not understand the importance of cultivating a team.

Let's quickly take a closer look at the definition of *Cultivate*:

Cultivate: cul·ti·vate (verb):

to promote or improve growth by labor and attention: to grow and care for: to grow or raise (something) under conditions you can control.

According to this definition, cultivating sounds like farming. Truth be told, the role of a leader is much like those of a farmer; someone who pays close attention to his crops and the surrounding elements that can positively or negatively effect their growth. In addition to focusing on the crops, paying keen attention to the environment will allow for a healthy harvest, while ensuring strong yields for years to come.

How important is cultivation to a farmer? About 150 plant species make up the world's food supply. More specifically, three "mega-crops" made up of: rice, wheat, and maize, account for over half of the world-wide food production. It would be fair to say the cultivation of these crops is of the greatest importance.

When a farmer fails to implement proper growing techniques, it can effect many lives. Over seven billion people populate the earth and the survival of the entire human race depends on our ability to produce enough food to sustain all of these lives. Unattended crops will fail to grow. Sound familiar? Furthermore, the neglect of the land will result in soil erosion, negatively impacting growth for future years.

Cultivation is not something to take lightly; for a farmer or a leader. When a leader fails to implement proper techniques to grow people, the negative impacts can be similar to that of farming. Farmers have techniques to provide proper cultivation: adding nutrients to the soil, composting, planting cover crops, and mulching.

In addition to being aware of the techniques available to cultivating a team, leaders must also watch out for the pitfalls.

## THE TRAINING TRAP

When I speak to leaders about the strategies they employ for building their teams, most proudly refer to some form of staff training they have scheduled, conducted, or recommended. While training has its merits, mistaking it for cultivating can lead to a dysfunctional team, lackluster results, and unwanted frustrations.

The problem with training is it is usually an attempt to fix everything that is wrong. Issues on the production line result in training classes, while problems in the sales department usher in new training programs. In most organizations, training is not held in the highest regard, often perceived synonymously with errors, mistakes, and reprimands.

Often implemented poorly, and rarely providing the long-term, permanent solutions it was intended for, most training falls short of its objectives. Worse yet, when it fails to fully resolve an issue, people begin to have the perception that it has little value. Because most training is designed to fix broken things, it does not make sense that this is your only team-building tactic.

Organizations spend hundreds of millions of dollars every year on training programs, yet they still experience the same mediocre results from their teams. When properly implemented, training is a viable way to increase knowledge. Cultivating, however, increases growth through teamwork, as it promotes deeper levels of learning and understanding.

**Training**      – Knowing More

**Cultivating**   – Growing More

Training is necessary in any organization. When done right, it creates higher levels of efficiency, increased confidence levels of team members, and greater customer satisfaction. When implementing any form of training in your organization, keep some basic techniques at the forefront of your program:

1.  Always have a definitive outcome

2.  Understand the specific needs of the student

3.  Provide regular follow up

Whether I was a young Marine, the vice president of a multi-million dollar company, or the owner of my own business, training has been and always will be a powerful tool for enhancing my performance and the performance of those around me. But my training programs fully support the cultivation of a team.

## STARTING TO CULTIVATE

Cultivation always starts at the top. Just as a farmer rises at the crack of dawn to tend to his fields, a leader must always be prepared to rise to the exciting challenge of cultivating the team. You do not need to put on a pair of overalls, hop on a tractor, and pop a piece of straw in your mouth to begin this process. But it just might leave a lasting impression on your team.

Cultivation, in a manner that fundamentally causes people to become better and improves their performance, will not be found in a training session. It will not be discovered in a PowerPoint presentation or in the pages of a handbook. Creating teamwork, in an environment of learning and understanding, is a process that takes place by consistently applying the ABC's of cultivation.

**The ABC's of Cultivating:**

    A.  Achieve Authenticity

    B.  Be the Beacon

    C.  Create Camaraderie

**Achieve Authenticity** – developing a team of people who are genuine, reliable, and dedicated is not as easy as it might seem. Leaders are not typically handed a dream team upon assuming a leadership position, but they are more than capable of developing one, provided they can achieve high levels of authenticity among all team members.

Creating an environment where people can be authentic, operating with trust and honesty, will develop team members who are able to perform naturally as part of a unit. Authenticity allows team members to provide honest feedback, leading to more viable solutions. Honesty leads to truth and truth brings forth integrity. Authenticity allows these characteristics to form the unbreakable foundation of your staff. Imagine having a team of genuine, trustworthy, honest, reliable, and dedicated people, all focused on common goals.

Achieving authenticity allows leaders to develop stronger teams, but it requires deeper levels of dialogue. It cannot be achieved solely through notes, letters, and e-mails. To raise teamwork to this level, leaders must engage in meaningful discussions with the team as a whole and each member individually.

Great leaders are great listeners. They use questions to gain a better understanding of their team members, their organizations, and the unique challenges within their environments. Leaders should be cautious about using questions that can be interpreted as forms of manipulation, interrogation, or finding fault.

Great teams are built upon open discussions, free from agendas and pressure. Striving for genuineness, leaders should use questions to build trust, loyalty, and respect. I ask questions, not because the answer is of the greatest importance, but because achieving authenticity is my highest priority. I ask questions like, "Can you share with me more about that?" "Do you have a solution?" and "What can we do better?"

Teams that operate with distrust and dissatisfaction tend to increase frustrations and negative behaviors throughout their organizations. Tracing the roots of their behaviors often points to the quality of the dialogue occurring within their teams. When leaders fail to develop deeper forms of dialogue, they will fail to achieve authenticity within their ranks.

Leaders who desire to understand situations better and allow their staff to share their own unique experiences, will open up lines of communication to help bond team members together with the perspective of discovering solutions.

**Leadership Link** Engage in deeper dialogue more often. Provide the support necessary to minimize conflicts and maximize results, together as a team.

**Be the Beacon** – to a ship at sea, navigating through a dark and foreboding storm, there is no greater sight than the beacon of a lighthouse. More than being a guide, it instantaneously fills the crew with hope and relief. As a leader, be the beacon for your team; the shining light of guidance and support.

Teams are usually assigned priority objectives, shouldering much of the workload and stress. They need leaders who project the illumination of positivity; not the spotlight of interrogation. Leaders are the guiding light, helping their people to stay focused on the mission and purpose behind their actions.

How do leaders stay focused on the vision of their organization, while trying to handle the myriad of details and requirements of leading a team? Invest time to share the big picture of your organization with your team members. Share the goals, the aspirations, and the greater purpose of why everyone has been united into a cohesive team.

To cultivate a team, leaders are required to inspire, motivate, and influence people. When their crew experiences a lack of clarity and a decrease in self-confidence, it is up to the leader to transform them into people with higher belief levels and increased commitment.

Keeping them focused on the big picture ensures that the small things do not become overwhelming roadblocks. Constantly sharing the greater purpose with your team will keep them moving forward, toward the important goals of the organization. But sharing the big picture is not only important for the team members; it is also important for the leaders.

It is easy to feel overwhelmed when you juggle many items and spin many plates. I have always found that focusing on the big picture provided me with the balance I needed to be a better leader for my team, and to constantly shine a light of guidance.

**Leadership Link**   Call daily meetings to review the big picture. Seize the opportunity to reset priorities as team members become re-energized with purpose, clarity, and conviction.

**Create Camaraderie** – as a U.S. Marine, I have experienced the highest levels of camaraderie. Training and preparing for combat develops a bond virtually impossible to duplicate in the civilian sector. I share a kindred spirit with my Marine brothers and sisters, and with my fellow veterans. This unbreakable bond is one of the things I miss the most from my service days. It is also one of the things I constantly seek out.

While your staff will not likely be facing enemy forces, creating camaraderie will take teamwork to an entirely new level for your organization. This bond does not occur because people get along. It does not happen by spending most of your day with someone, nor is it merely the spirit of good fellowship.

True camaraderie is the mutual trust and friendship that evolves between people who believe wholeheartedly in their purpose, and overcome the challenges they face together, while fully engaged in their mission. To achieve this level of teamwork requires leaders to do more than just promote corporate activities such as sports teams and community service events.

The bond that develops deep levels of loyalty, dedication, and commitment can only be achieved by challenging the team. But most leaders try to avoid this technique, fearing backlash from their staff. Here is a little leadership secret: great teams want to be challenged, and they have a tremendous amount of respect for the leader who believes in them enough to create the opportunities for them to grow.

Team members want to be inspired, motivated, and influenced. They want to look forward to showing up every day and creating new ideas. Leaders must not set impossible challenges, but rather pay particular attention to setting achievable benchmarks that will cause each member of their teams to develop, personally and professionally.

Leaders possess the ability to influence people. Why waste that gift? Never keep a team at mediocrity. Challenge them to do things they do not believe they can do. Leaders do more than provide motivation: they provide opportunities to step up to the next level. Challenging your team is not just a reflection of your belief in them, but also your belief in yourself.

Begin by assigning smaller, challenging projects to your team and allow them to display their creativity and initiative. Set timelines and help to keep them on track. Overcoming challenges together creates a strong bond and transforms your staff from spectators to team players.

Give your team a chance to grow, and they will provide you with opportunities to do it more often. Yes, there is always a risk involved when you issue challenges. You are probably qualified to do it faster, do it better, and do it with less stress. But your role as a leader is to cultivate a team. You cannot successfully take everything on yourself, and hope to build deep bonds among your team. You cultivate a team by creating camaraderie.

**Leadership Link** Encourage your team to work together, sharing ideas and discovering the best solutions.

Cultivating a team is typically a new discipline for many leaders. It will take time to become natural at cultivating the individuals on your team, but the results will be well worth your efforts. Cultivating allows your team to grow. Most importantly, cultivating leads to collaborating.

# CHAPTER 9

## COLLABORATION

*Unleash the Power of People.*

From the outside, my daughter's preschool was peaceful and tranquil, beautiful and inviting. But as I entered the building to drop her off, I encountered an eruption of chaos; a mixture of talking, crying, laughing, and the sound of toys crashing to the floor. In her classroom, the communication elevated as I was surrounded by four year olds, all determined to be the first to share their vitally important stories with me.

Taking my daughter to school provided me with a unique insight into the challenges of getting people to work together; to collaborate. The whirlwind of uncontrolled dialogue and energy I witnessed each day made me question if I could last more than fifteen minutes in a room filled with these toddlers. The answer was important because I was scheduled to volunteer as a "teacher's assistant" one upcoming morning.

The day rolled around and I somewhat reluctantly reported for duty. I admit I had some reservations, perhaps some anxiety about stepping into an environment with no structure, but a free-for-all of attitudes and emotions. Does that sound like any work environments you have experienced?

As expected, chaos ensued. But to my surprise, it only lasted for about the first 15-20 minutes. Once the impact of being dropped off had subsided, I watched a group of people begin the process of collaboration. Influencing others, they placed a great emphasis on encouraging the group to see things from a new point of view. They also provided support to help in the achievement of better results. The teachers did a great job too, but I am referring to the efforts of the four year olds who operated in a powerful environment of collaboration.

With the guidance of their teachers, the children accomplished amazing works of art, towering structures of blocks, and physics-defying forts. They might not have gotten along every step of the way, but they produced incredible results. The preschoolers worked together toward a greater purpose, even if they were the only ones who understood the purpose.

After three hours, I came out with a different perspective on working together. I also developed a much deeper appreciation for the teachers and the patience they displayed with their tiny teams. They used their position of leadership to do more than just show the children how to cooperate and coordinate their efforts. They encouraged them to collaborate and achieve something new.

The teachers taught them how to work together as a team and create something greater than their individual efforts could have produced. If collaboration can be achieved with four year olds, it can most certainly be implemented in any organization. The benefits of fostering innovative results will have a long-term impact – on the team, the leaders, and the company.

**The Benefits of Collaboration:**
1. Supports organizational goals
2. Enhances team member strengths
3. Promotes forward-thinking
4. Increases an organization's relevancy

The benefits of collaboration are overwhelmingly positive. But achieving and maintaining an environment that promotes high-level results through creativity and innovation is difficult to achieve unless an understanding of authentic collaboration can be attained.

## UNDERSTANDING COLLABORATION

A lack of collaboration is costly to an organization and draining to its team members. Most leaders spend the majority of their time dealing with internal conflicts and problems. Meetings become a frustrating exercise in mistake-management, accounting for endless hours of repetitive discussion, with little-to-no resolution.

Most leaders whom I work with dedicate at least 50 percent of their time to handling the resolution of conflicts and customer satisfaction issues. If a leader earns $100,000 per year, the organization is paying upwards of $50,000 annually toward these activities, and losing much more in missed opportunities.

Unfortunately, the high cost of a non-collaborative environment does not stop there. Organizations typically experience greater employee turnover and the loss of top talent. The expense of replacing a team member is often three to five times the cost of their annual salary. Without enthusiasm in the workplace, employees often have higher levels of absenteeism and lower levels of production.

Creating a collaborative environment will produce an immediate ROI as leaders dedicate their time to productive solutions that will eliminate the need for time-wasting activities, and will support an exciting environment of creativity, growth, and success. This collaborative ROI comes from new opportunities, cost reductions, team optimization, and solid business decisions.

By now, every leader reading this book should be jumping at the opportunity to implement this strategy within their organization, right? Unfortunately, many fail to sustain this type of environment because they do not understand collaboration, often confusing it with cooperation and coordination.

**Coordination** – the process of exchanging information and resources between individuals, teams, and organizations to accomplish a mutual objective. This process requires attention to detail and follow through, but does not strive to create something new through innovation.

Example: when a customer places and order, a team member coordinates its fulfillment with the supplier.

**Cooperation** – the ability for individuals to work together as a team for the completion of a common objective. This process requires teamwork and positive attitudes, but does not strive to develop new systems to enhance results.

Example: when an order encounters an issue, team members cooperate to ensure that the objective is achieved.

**Collaboration** – the collective creative energies generated by linking together the members of a team who are dedicated to uncovering new, innovative ideas for success and growth. This process requires a leader, a team, and an environment dedicated to supporting creativity and innovation.

Example: when ideas are needed to elevate customer satisfaction, and add depth to an organization's products, resources, and services, team members collaborate to discover viable solutions.

In addition to making the distinction between coordination and cooperation, leaders must also identify the enemy of collaboration and avoid it at all costs. I have found many leaders sacrifice collaboration for consensus; striving to make everyone "feel" good. Collaboration does not require everyone to agree; it does require everyone to set their sights on the greater solution, in an environment of trust and respect.

A collaborative team does not strive to make friendships; it strives to make advancements. Proper collaboration, however, will produce camaraderie between the members of the team. But when consensus overrides collaboration, possibilities are reduced to compromises. Consensus often slows down momentum, and allows sub-par ideas to make it through the collaborative filters.

Authentic collaboration is not easy to achieve, but it is absolutely worth the effort that will be put forth. Creating something that is larger than the individual efforts of each member provides a heightened sense of satisfaction and connects each person on the team at a deeper level. Being part of a collaborative team is an exhilarating, life-changing feeling.

## THE LINK TO COLLABORATION

Creating and maintaining a collaborative environment might seem like a daunting task. But it is the result of transferring energy and power, from the leader to the team, in a way that creates increased momentum. To achieve the win-win results of "pulling" a team together for a higher purpose, let's take a quick look at the elements required to pull a freight train.

An average locomotive engine might pull 100 train cars, each weighing 50 tons. That is 5,000 tons or 10 million pounds. The idea of getting a train with smooth wheels, on a smooth track, to gain enough traction to move could seem impossible. But it happens every day. Not only do these trains gain enough momentum to move forward, but they can travel at speeds of over 60 mph. The ability to pull this amount of weight involves the collective effort of each train car.

Without getting too deep into physics and the difference between static and kinetic friction, we will explore the connection between the engine and the boxcars, which allows the insurmountable weight of a freight train to start moving, pick up speed, and become virtually an unstoppable force.

One of the most important components of a train is the coupling; the "link" between the cars. So how important is the link? The connection between each car must allow for movement – a range of motion. *Slack action* is the term used to describe the amount of free movement of one freight car before it transmits its motion to an adjoined car. If the connection is too rigid, it will prohibit any movement.

Motion results from keeping the cars loosely coupled, which allows trains to bend around dangerous curves, and is a vital component of starting the initial momentum. As the engine starts to move, the power of the locomotive transfers to each car, creating a wave of compressing couplings between all of the cars. One at a time, they begin to move, causing motion in the other cars. The calculated space between the couplings allows for this movement and the transfer of power.

If all of the cars were connected with a rigid, unmoving link, even a train with a powerful engine would fail to pull the weight behind it. The link of connected cars would merely become one large solid object, remaining motionless on the tracks, despite the engine exhorting massive energy.

Like a fast moving train, collaboration will take a lot of energy to get it started, but it is often impossible to stop the positive, forward-moving momentum, once it achieves high velocity. A leader is like a locomotive engine, building the momentum and outputting the energy needed to maintain movement in the right direction. A leader is the first link in creating the collaborative environment in their organization.

I first experienced collaboration as a newly promoted Lance Corporal. One might think the Marine Corps has too rigid an environment for collaboration, but nothing could be farther from the truth. In 1988, I was deployed to the desert of Twentynine Palms, CA, to participate in Operation Gallant Eagle.

In the sweltering heat, I joined thousands of other Marines for a two week joint operation with the Army. This exercise provided soldiers and Marines the opportunity to perform in a collaborative environment involving tactics and warfare. It was a massive operation, with battalions of infantry and air wing commands.

Our leaders provided the opportunity for the troops to practice their existing procedures, while developing new strategies and techniques. This collaborative effort, allowed the Army and the Marine Corps to "battle" each other, with the outcome of achieving higher effectiveness and efficiencies for both sides. Who won the battle? Well, the answer is probably based on who you ask. According to the soldiers, the Army won. According to the Marines, the Marine Corps won. With collaboration, both sides ultimately won important victories for their organizations.

**Leadership Link**  The outcome of collaboration is not just collaborating. The outcome is to achieve greater results.

## THE THINK TANK

So, you're sold on the idea of collaboration and the benefits it will bring to you, your team, and your organization. Understanding the power of making the leadership link to this fast-moving train is the first step. But how do you get it to leave the station?

A leader must establish the framework for collaboration in their environment. Merely pulling some people together to discuss things will not get the job done. Sustained, collaborative results require the formation of a Think Tank; a forward-thinking team that brings authenticity, trust, experience, and passion.

Specific keys must be used to unlock a solution-oriented team in order to yield amazing, insightful, and valuable results.

**The Keys to a Successful Think Tank:**

1. Membership must be earned
2. Objectives must be crystal clear
3. Time frames must be established
4. Schedules must be set

**Membership** – membership should be earned, never given. Form a think tank, comprised of your strongest leaders, not your best friends. Collaboration teams only work if every person brings their "A" game to the table. As their leader, it is your responsibility to form the team.

Members need to exhibit the highest levels of respect for each other, understanding that their collective input is what will help each of them to arrive at the desired solution.

**Objectives** – every think tank serves a purpose, and should have an outcome, which must be clearly communicated to each member of the team. Their role in the think tank should be directly linked to the objectives. By focusing on the objectives, a leader can eliminate the personal egos of the team members, and increase the results from their professional input. By clearly articulating the objective, you will ignite inspiration. Passion and dedication are contagious.

**Time Frames** – setting time frames creates a sense of urgency. If the outcome is important enough to form a think tank, it is important enough to have timelines. Some time frames might be non-negotiable. If your think tank is unable to provide a solution by a specific date, you might lose a sale, or a customer.

Some timelines might be more forgiving. But to show the outcome is important, establish time frames for all think tank objectives.

**Schedules** – each think tank is typically comprised of leaders and top talent who already have a full plate. Setting up a schedule for collaboration will allow you to harness time mastery and keep your think tank team members from feeling overwhelmed.

Schedule the team to regularly review and evaluate the effectiveness of their efforts. Schedules allow for balance by setting specific durations for each meeting.

## STARTING A THINK TANK

The impact of collaboration cannot be understated. Studies show that the collaborative process can dramatically affect profitability, team member performance, growth, sales results, product development, customer satisfaction, and overall quality. Authentic collaboration is a key driver of success, and particular attention should be paid to properly starting a solution-oriented team.

Providing the free-flowing innovation of ideas in a structured format requires a leader who is confident and creative. Leaders who are accustomed to a traditional "command and control" leadership style might find the collaborative process foreign to their way of operating, unless they can make the necessary shifts. Rigid leaders will have difficulty achieving consistent collaboration.

To benefit from the collaborative efforts of a think tank, the starting steps are crucial. If you have never put together a team of innovative thinkers, you might want to start small, gathering the team to work on specific projects and assignments. Before tackling highly technical objectives, I formed a think tank to discover permanent solutions to some of our internal workflow issues.

Focusing on improving our internal efficiencies, our collaborative team learned how to work together, as we discovered out-of-the-box solutions to our own issues. As we shared innovative ideas, we focused on the creation of a checkpoint system to reduce errors made by our staff. By starting small, and then isolating our collaborative energies, we launched a system that reduced our errors by nearly 98 percent.

Regardless of the scope of the team's objectives, collaboration must always start at the top and have the full support of the entire leadership team. The actions and the words of the senior leaders will have a major impact on the innovative results the team achieves.

Collaborative teams must also be surrounded by trust and respect. Leaders should provide regular constructive feedback to the entire team to ensure they are on target with the assigned objectives. Trust will allow for crystal-clear communication in a safe environment; an environment that welcomes new ideas, no matter how bold or crazy.

Leaders should expect that certain contributions will cause some levels of disagreement and be prepared to resolve conflict in a fair and productive manner. You will always get more out of authentic collaboration than you were expecting. In addition to fresh, new ideas, collaboration empowers everyone involved, directly and indirectly.

While teamwork is a cornerstone of collaboration, collaboration helps to make each member of the team stronger.

## *THE POWER OF A THINK TANK*

Collaboration exponentially increases the odds of achieving organizational growth, as it positions leaders to work "on" important objectives. In today's fast-moving business environments, leaders need an edge. Those who are able to establish collaborative teams, replacing uncertainty with clarity, and developing new ideas for success, gain that edge.

As a vice president in the media industry, I watched businesses rise and fall, based on their relevancy as technology constantly evolved. In 2009, most of our clients began the transition from standard definition to high definition formats for their broadcast projects; those airing on television and cable networks.

While the picture quality became a visually superior image, high definition (HD) broadcasting presented many new variables which caused the transition to be more than a simple one-step process. Expensive new equipment and software presented additional learning curves. Many factors needed to be considered in order to achieve the desired results. Because this format was still relatively new, few experts worked in this area.

We needed to quickly elevate our relevancy to clients, if we expected them to remain our clients. The importance of our think tank grew as we addressed the upcoming technology trends. We identified our clients who would need HD services, the equipment required, and what our obstacles would be. Most importantly, we aimed for viable solutions we could present to all of our clients.

For a few years, we had been servicing the "deliverable" media needs for South Park, the highest rated show for the Comedy Central Network. Deliverables are the final copies of the show, and would be duplicated on various standard definition formats. We successfully fulfilled every weekly order, but they were on standard definition. The game was changing and I knew the South Park team would be transitioning to high definition soon.

Not wanting to fall behind the technology curve, I took a proactive approach and called on my think tank team. Together, we discussed a strategy and designed specific options I could present to my client. I did not take for granted that their HD business would come to us. I wanted to guarantee we worked to earn it. Southpark needed to go to where the HD solutions were. I needed us to be that place.

After flushing out all of the variables, possible obstacles, and challenges, I confidently contacted their post-production supervisor and suggested we run a series of tests for their transition to high definition broadcasting. After the collective data was gathered, the South Park team made their decision.

On March 11, 2009, South Park aired episode 182 in HD. Not only did we continue to service all of their media deliverable needs, we also took their entire library of past episodes and up-converted everything to HD. By enlisting the innovative and creative input of our think tank, the collaborative process allowed us to do more than just earn more business, it allowed us to transform our entire organization, empowering our people in the process.

# PART IV

## EXCEED POSSIBILITIES

# PART IV

## EXCEED POSSIBILITIES

*Organizations Do Not Fail; Leaders Do.*

Ask the members of any organization one simple question, "What should a leader do?" and you will discover a multitude of answers. Every team member, peer, and supervisor will have a different set of explanations on the true purpose of a leader. Leaders set goals; they motivate; they guide; they set strategy; they develop culture; they support. Leaders are expected to do all of this and more.

But one response quickly sums up what a leader is ultimately responsible for: *results*. In many organizations, the desired results might not clearly be identified and the pressure of "hitting the target" can be overwhelming. In today's highly competitive and unstable environment, successful leaders must strive to do more than just achieve results.

Doing things better than the competition is rarely enough. Strong leaders position themselves to exceed possibilities, enabling their organizations to attain new opportunities and avoid potential threats. Leaders are responsible for hitting the target. Those who lack the necessary accuracy, might soon find themselves looking for work elsewhere.

Black Monday is the unofficial term used for the day of reckoning in the National Football League. Following the final Sunday of the NFL's regular season, numerous coaches and general managers no longer hold the same positions of leadership they held the day before. They are fired; released from their organizations based on their inability to achieve the desired results.

The quality of leadership in an organization, more than any other component, determines success and failure. Leaders must be able to identify the target, achieve results, and exceed possibilities. Learning to hone your skills will improve your chances for success.

## AIMING FOR SUCCESS

I slowly raised the barrel of my rifle, lining up my front sight post over the target in front of me. Mounted in large wooden frames, the paper targets featured various sizes and shapes, based on the distance from the impact zone. Two targets, the "B-Mod" and the "Dog," resembled the upper-torso of a person, while another, the "Able," featured various size circles.

The outer circle of the Able target had the widest radius, but offered the least amount of points for striking inside of it. Each successive circle featured a smaller radius, but the number of points that could be earned increased. At the center of the target was the main objective – a solid black circle, twelve inches in diameter, worth the maximum of five points.

My results on the rifle range would do more than just qualify me as a rifleman. They would be an important step toward earning the title of U.S. Marine. At the first qualifying distance of 200 yards, the targets still seemed to be at a challenging distance to achieve the accuracy needed. But the 200-yard range was only the first test. I would soon move back to the 300-yard and 500-yard ranges.

I wanted to do more than just hit the target; I wanted as many bullseyes as I could get. To achieve consistent accuracy, we were taught how to achieve our battlesight zero (BZO). Perhaps the most important concept we learned was the sight settings placed on our rifles that would allow us to accurately fire our weapons in a "no-wind" condition. As we encountered external challenges that would affect our accuracy, such as weather and wind conditions, we would be able to make quick adjustments to improve our aim.

Determining a proper battlesight zero is crucial in combat as it allows Marines to engage an enemy threat without spending life-saving time to continually adjust the elevation of their iron sight posts. As a business leader, your ability to achieve consistent accuracy, despite any possible threat or exterior condition, is vital for your survival.

It should come as no surprise that the Corps provides each Marine with strategies, techniques, and resources to qualify as a rifleman. Every Marine is issued a Data Book; a journal of every shot fired. This allows for course-corrections, by making necessary adjustments to the rifle.

Weapon maintenance is held in the highest regard. Marines field strip their rifles and do a thorough cleaning, which ensures that their weapons work properly and affords them the greatest chances for accuracy and survival. When your life is on the line, you embrace every opportunity you can to exceed expectations.

## *SET YOUR SIGHTS ON SUCCESS*

What are you aiming for?

What are you doing to ensure that your accuracy stays on par with your organizational requirements?

Have you determined your Leadership Sight Zero (LZO)? Setting your LZO will help to improve your focus, your accuracy, and your results.

But where do you start?

An abundance of leadership training programs and "expert" advice is available for today's aspiring leaders. Yet predictable results still elude many organizations. Hitting the target might often seem impossible. But with the right approach, not only will you hit the target, you will exceed possibilities. By focusing on the correct techniques, leaders increase their ability to yield positive results, positioning themselves, and their teams, to pull off the impossible.

Based on the organizational challenges faced by many leaders, such as poor infrastructure, weak corporate culture, and lackluster performance, achieving basic results can often seem like a daunting task. With overwhelming circumstances, the idea of exceeding possibilities might not even appear as a distant blip on the radar for most leaders.

Regardless of their struggles, leaders are judged on their ability to identify and achieve the necessary results to move their organizations forward and upward. Anything less can paralyze an organization, destroy momentum, and create uncertainty among team members. Failure is not an option for a leader.

**Leadership Link** Leaders who can exceed possibilities, uniquely position themselves for great opportunities for growth.

## START NOW

The need for strong leaders has never been greater, but the number of leaders able to achieve sustainable results has never been lower. Leaders are rarely issued magic wands, crystal balls, or a book of spells. Yet daily, they are expected to pull off the impossible. They rarely receive much guidance, and the expectations placed upon them often feel insurmountable.

When I began to assume leadership duties at the post-production company, I was aware of the internal components we needed to address and improve. Our culture was in need of an overhaul, a better workflow was required, and a more aggressive sales strategy was long overdue. The desired results had been identified to increase our revenue by 50 percent, which was no small task, especially in a highly technical industry that was evolving almost daily.

I did more than merely set out to achieve 50 percent greater sales results. I was determined to exceed possibilities by striving for over 100 percent growth. My goal was not without merit. I analyzed our current industry environment, assessed our competition, and determined that our internal weaknesses could become significant strengths. I created a plan, developed a leadership team, and consistently stretched the vision of everyone in our organization.

What were my results? Within eighteen months, I had been promoted from an entry-level scheduler to the operations supervisor, to the facility manager, and finally to the vice president of the entire company. But these promotions did not occur solely because we achieved our desired results, they happened because we exceeded possibilities.

Our annual revenue soared to over 300 percent. Because of increased efficiencies, we also experienced greater profit margins and higher levels of customer satisfaction. The opportunities for growth opened up for everyone on our team. Personal and professional development ushered in promotions and raises for many team members.

This level of growth did not happen by accident, nor did it happen by merely striving for better results. It occurred because I systematically applied three key principles that allowed me to set my Leadership Sight Zero (LZO), and regularly exceed possibilities.

**The Three Keys to Set Your LZO and Exceed Possibilities:**

1. Have a plan
2. Build leaders
3. Become a visionary leader

As a leader, I have always understood that my core responsibility was to achieve the results set forth by the organization. As a successful leader, I have to constantly establish my Leadership Sight Zero and focus on more than the results. I set my sights on exceeding possibilities. If I aim for the "impossible," I know my results will hit the target.

At the end of the day, leaders are judged predominantly on what they have achieved. Good intentions and a great personality only go so far. Creating a strategic plan, developing strong leaders, and becoming a visionary leader, will do much more than enable you to achieve results – you will exceed possibilities.

# CHAPTER 10

## HAVE A PLAN

*Stop Winging It.*

Today is going to be a great day. You can just feel it. You leave your house, slightly ahead of schedule. You confidently step up to your car and take your keys out of your pocket. Opening the door, you envision the extraordinary results that lay ahead. Ready to seize the day, you put your key into the ignition and give it a turn. Nothing happens. Not a sputter; not a clank. You try again. Nothing happens. You try once more. Again, the engine fails to start, and your excitement about the day has all but vanished.

There are few things as frustrating as a car that will not start, especially when you need to get somewhere important. With the anticipation of driving their teams to greater results, every leader needs to go somewhere important, too. Unfortunately, most never make it out of the parking lot. Not because they lack the skills, but because they lack a plan.

Without a plan, leaders are often paralyzed, unable to move their organizations in the right direction. Deciding to achieve better results is a wise choice, but good intentions will not take leaders to where they need to go. They need a plan to make their desires a reality.

When I ask leaders to show me their plan for achieving success, my question is usually followed by an awkward silence. As they explain why they do not have a formal plan for growth, I inquire about anything they might have put together to grow their organization; a basic outline or even some notes. Again, nothing.

Like a car that won't start, a leader without a plan remains motionless and silent. Those who are not able to help their organizations to achieve greater levels of success are often left frustrated and discouraged. Turning the key and failing to achieve results can be devastating, but your journey to success does not need to stay like that.

I rarely have difficulty finding leaders with great intentions. But finding leaders who have mapped out the strategic and tactical components necessary for sustainable growth is a different story. Too many leaders try to develop their organizations without putting together a plan to help guide them and keep them on track.

## IMPROVING YOUR TIME

Just days before graduating from boot camp, the recruits of Platoon 1095 completed their final Physical Fitness Test (PFT). In addition to all of the sit-ups and pull-ups, we were required to run three miles in less than twenty-eight minutes. I am not a runner, so the idea of running three miles was a bit intimidating. But the challenge of doing it within such a time frame seemed nearly impossible.

I soon discovered, exceeding possibilities was not a suggestion in the Marine Corps. It was part of their plan. The first time our drill instructors took us on a run, we probably ran a mile or less. But it felt like the full three miles, maybe a little more. I struggled to keep up my pace, and was completely winded when we finished the brief run. My only thought was, "If I had difficulty with one mile, how could I possibly do three miles in less than twenty-eight minutes?"

For our transformation into U.S. Marines, our daily training was filled with many challenging objectives. Running was just one of them. Every minute of every day was meticulously planned out by our drill instructors, and with our graduation day rapidly approaching, they left nothing to chance. We were not always privy to every detail in their plan, but knowing they had one, changed all of our belief levels.

Occasionally, we would catch a quick glimpse of their plan. Each drill instructor kept a small index card with him, detailing all of the daily activities that would keep us headed in the right direction with our training. Detailed planning ensured that we did not miss any of the steps needed for our growth and development, including our ability to complete a three-mile run.

After weeks of sticking to the plan, I was ready to tackle my running challenge. Crossing the finish line, in the alloted time was another step to becoming one of the few; one of the proud. It would help me to become a United States Marine.

Checking his stopwatch, Sergeant Hughes yelled out my final time as I crossed the finish line. I did better than run three miles in the required time, I ran three miles in eighteen minutes and fifty seconds. I not only achieved my desired results, but I surpassed my own possibilities. Our leaders did not take their mission lightly, nor did they wing it or merely rely on hope. Leaders in the United States Marine Corps use a plan to guarantee the success of their teams.

## THE NEED FOR A PLAN

Nearly twelve years after my tour of duty with the Marine Corps ended, I found myself again relying on the power of a plan to achieve results. As a newly promoted leader at the post-production company, it was time to share the goal of increasing our annual revenue by 50 percent. The team's reaction was less than enthusiastic.

They immediately focused on how busy they already were, and pointed out that we would need more staff, more resources, more everything. Because our current workload seemed difficult to manage, the idea of increasing it seemed impossible. But leaders should strive for exceeding possibilities, right?

My team's belief level would not allow them to see our true potential. I believed we were capable of increasing sales by more than 50 percent. After a closer look at our missed opportunities, I projected we could achieve 100 percent growth. But if my team failed to even believe we could achieve 50 percent, how could they wrap their heads around the idea of 100 percent?

Before sharing my goal of 100 percent with them, I needed more than mere words of inspiration. I needed something they could see; something that could clarify my vision and remove their excuses. I needed a solid plan. Success might start with vision, but results are achieved only by a team dedicated to following a plan.

Based on the needs of each individual organization, plans can vary drastically in size and scope. Deciding which type of plan will best serve the goals of your organization can often be challenging. Understanding the purpose of specific types of plans will allow you to combine elements from each, customizing a plan that best suits your needs.

Here is a brief overview of some of the most common forms of plans used for growing and developing organizations:

**Business Plan** – often used for start-up purposes and to provide exit strategies. Business plans are typically used to acquire additional funding from banks and other investors.

**Strategic Plan** – involves analyzing new opportunities, competition, and possible challenges. Strategic plans seek to maximize the strengths and minimize the weaknesses of the organization, while determining how to position the team for greater effectiveness.

**Tactical Plan** – short-term in nature, these plans focus on developing immediate actionable items that will support any long-term planning. They increase the involvement of mid-level leaders and their team members to improve workflow and customer service.

**Operational Plan** – also short-term in nature, operational plans focus on improving the efficiencies and effectiveness of specific departments, as they relate to the overall long-term goals of the organization. They might involve restructuring, especially as it relates to the quality of the staff.

**Financial Plan** – the elements that determine how an organization will afford to achieve its goals and objectives. Financial plans are typically created after the organizational objectives have been set. Financial plans establish timeframes and lists the staff, resources, equipment, and materials needed to achieve these objectives.

## STARTING YOUR PLAN

Perhaps the greatest stumbling block for most leaders is the starting point. How do you begin to develop a plan that encompasses so much? Think of your plan as a written description of your organization's current status and future aspirations. The bulk of the content will focus around the action items necessary to get from point A to point B. Sounds easy enough?

If you jot down a few lines on the back of a napkin at a restaurant, you have started to write your plan. Fortunately, your plan does not need to be 100 percent complete to start enjoying the rewards. The process of starting a plan often unifies members of your team, especially as you include them in the development process.

While at lunch to discuss the completion of Pixar's animated film, *Toy Story*, director, John Lasseter, and three writers asked the question, "What's next?" Their question led to more than just some sketches on the back of a napkin. It began the planning process for some of Pixar's next films: *A Bug's Life*, *Monsters, Inc.*, *Finding Nemo*, and *Wall-E*.

These four films grossed nearly $2.5 billion in ticket sales alone, not including additional merchandise such as toys and DVDs. Nor does it include any sequels to these huge hits. Great things can be accomplished when you take the time to formulate your plan. What could you accomplish if you took the time to start yours?

I was not an expert in plan-writing. The plan I initially constructed probably looked like some amateur sketches, but it ultimately focused on the basic elements needed for growth. I tweaked, changed, and updated our plan at least a dozen times during our growth phase. Not only did this plan help us to achieve the goal of 50 percent growth and accomplish my vision of 100 percent growth, it allowed us to increase our annual revenue by over 300 percent.

Here is the basic outline I used to develop a viable plan for predictable growth:

**Overview of your Organization** – I started with a brief history of our company, then detailed our current products and services. I also included potential future products and services we would offer. Most importantly, I identified "why" customers should choose us. Lastly, I incorporated our mission and vision statement, core values, and a description of our culture.

**Leadership Team** – in this section, I included a brief bio on each member of our leadership team. This caused an immediate interest from my leaders and I found that they were more engaged in helping me to complete the plan, knowing they were an integral part of it.

**Organizational Goals** – dream big and list out all of the long-term goals that will allow your organization to achieve success. It is okay that some might seem impossible to reach. Next, break your important long-term goals into smaller, short-term goals that can be accomplished in ninety-day intervals.

**Priority Objectives** – take a closer look at your short-term goals, identifying all of the high priority objectives and important tasks that need to be achieved to put you on track for success. A list of action items, with time frames you can track, needs to be established.

**Strategic Enhancements** – looking at your organization from a bird's eye view, identify the key enhancements and changes that need to be made to allow your plan to succeed. You might need to restructure your team, redesign specific departments, implement new software, and update policies and procedures.

**Strategies for Growth** – planning and training go hand in hand. A plan that predicts growth must also map out the training necessary to prepare the team for success. You might need to create and implement programs in your sales department, with your leadership team, and with your entire staff to increase their knowledge and skills.

**Budget** – identify all anticipated expenses to support the growth of your organization. Factor in an increase in staff and additional resources. Set budgetary goals that will help to minimize expenses while focusing on greater returns. Increased profit margins should be a goal.

**Conclusion** – sum up the benefits of achieving the results for which you are striving. How will this plan impact the organization, its culture, and the lives of the team? Make it personal to increase relevancy to the people on your team.

You do not need to be an expert in writing plans to create a plan that will help you to exceed possibilities. Planning is about developing a better understanding of your organization. In its most simplistic form, it describes where you are, where you need to go, and exactly how to get there.

The initial plan I developed was far from perfect, but it enabled progress by unifying our team with clarity and purpose. To the best of my abilities, I projected out our next three years. With our end goal in mind, we launched our plan and focused our efforts intensely on the first ninety days. We used this block of time as an opportunity to harness our skills and course-correct our progress.

## THE BENEFITS OF A PLAN

I often witness leaders working relentlessly on the "busy work" of their business. They miss out on the opportunity to create a plan that will shift everyone's focus onto the big picture of the organization and the actions necessary for growth. This mis-guided focus can be one of the biggest mistakes leaders make.

Because every organization is at different stages in their development, each plan must be customized to encapsulate where the business is, and where it needs to go. Some organizations require more attention to leadership development, while others need additional sales training. Some need to streamline their workflow, while others need expand their product line.

Regardless of where your organization currently stands, there are significant benefits to having a plan; benefits that will begin to move your organization forward. Providing direction, motivation, and creativity is not all you will receive from a plan.

**The Benefits of Having a Plan:**

1. Planning increases buy-in

2. Planning opens new opportunities

3. Planning moves the future closer

To experience the benefits of a plan, leaders must be committed to the detailed development, the implementation, and the continuous course-correction needed to achieve high level results.

## Planning Increases Buy-In

The high aspirations of leaders do not always have the desired effect on their teams. Powerful goals, prioritized objectives, and important tasks might fail to gain traction if the team is not completely connected to the projected results. Because most people associate growth with additional workload, they are often hesitant to voluntarily take on new projects.

The process of planning increases the buy-in from the team by outlining the organization's mission with a detailed roadmap for success, allowing team members to see the direction and the destination. If possible, involve your team in the development of the plan, or at least specific components. Involvement fosters additional buy-in.

Buy-in increases as leaders articulate each team member's connection with the plan and what will be expected of them. Planning makes your team stronger by tapping into their strengths and providing the necessary training to minimize their weaknesses.

**Leadership Link** Invest time with your team. Involve them in the development of the plan, and share with them the progress being made.

## Planning Opens New Opportunities

Many leaders are often charismatic, inspirational, and influential. Team members might be captivated by their personalities, but not truly understand their directions. Unfortunately, neither do those leaders. When leaders fail to plan, more is lost than just the desired results.

- Planning opens new opportunities that would have otherwise, never been imaginable.

- Planning ahead enables leaders to do more than just share their vision, it enables people to bring their A-game to the table.

- Planning promotes high-level collaboration, which allows people to hone their skills and maximize their resources.

- Planning gets people involved in discovering solutions, which is when the real magic starts.

- Planning allows an organization to be bigger than the collective efforts of just one person, by ushering in new ideas. New ideas create new opportunities that allow the plan to achieve results faster and more effectively.

**Leadership Link** Encourage team members to discuss specific components of the plan and support their collaborative efforts. New opportunities will open.

## Planning Moves the Future Closer

Working with many business leaders on their plans, I have found a bit of reluctance when initially setting time frames for long-term goals. Understandably, most leaders do not want to over promise and under-deliver.

Planning increases efficiencies and effectiveness, taking into account all of the aspects of an organization and how they relate to one other. Looking at the business in this manner encourages the elimination of the components that do not support the greater vision. The benefits of planning actually helps leaders to position themselves to move future dates closer as more short-term goals are accomplished, usually ahead of schedule.

Create a long-term vision, even if you cannot fully see it in its final view. Dream a little and think big, projecting out at least a few years. Focus on where you need to be in three to five; not what appears to be realistic. Stretching your vision will allow your organization to move into new territories, both nationally and internationally. It will also allow you to be cognizant of the necessary steps to get there.

**Leadership Link**  Invest time with your team. Involve them in the development of the plan, and share with them the progress being made.

## SLOW DOWN TO SPEED UP

By not investing the necessary time to develop a plan for growth, leaders often find themselves resolving ongoing issues and fighting fires, rather than moving their organization along the path of success. Planning holds leaders accountable, and allows them to become proactive with the goals of their organization.

Take the time to plan. Slow down so you and your team can speed up; the right way. Plans hold us accountable and allow us to course-correct, which is inherently important, especially with the many competing distractions and challenges we face in our daily lives.

Most leaders want to achieve greater results; they want to exceed possibilities. But they have no roadmap to guide themselves and their teams in the right direction. Avoid unnecessary turmoil by mapping out your destination ahead of time. Stay a step ahead of your competition and position your organization for the impossible.

# CHAPTER 11

## BUILD LEADERS

*Developing Strong Leaders is Your Business.*

Putting together a plan for growth in your organization is an enlightening experience. But the implementation and execution of the plan will rest on the shoulders of all leaders in your organization. How important is it to build leaders? A strong leader can transform a weak plan into success, but a weak leader will minimize the impact of even the strongest plan.

Developing effective leadership, at all levels across the organization, will return significant value. Building leaders is the greatest security system you can install within your organization. In addition to helping to carry out your plan, leaders help protect your organization from the constant attack of the competition. New products, lower prices, and exciting marketing campaigns are just a few ways the competition can strike.

The most fatal blow to an organization comes as members of its team are hired away. But competitors rarely go after your under-performers. They set their sights on those who achieve results; those who can exceed possibilities. Leaders are under constant observation. You can be assured your competition is sizing them up, and determining how your leaders can help their own organizations to grow.

Losing a leader to a competitor is a highly damaging mistake. It is estimated that this can cost an organization two to three times the annual salary of that leader, if he decides to hang his hat with your competition. Most leaders do not leave their jobs solely because they can make more money elsewhere. They leave because they feel under appreciated and/or they perceive there is greater opportunity for growth elsewhere.

Losing a leader can have a significant impact on the organization, affecting workload, employee morale, and customer satisfaction. The departure of a key leader can send a negative message throughout your organization and to your customers, dramatically hindering your efforts for growth. Before your leaders leave to re-build themselves elsewhere, invest the time necessary to build them while they are still on your team.

## PRACTICE LEADERSHIP

Every organization is built upon the leadership capabilities of their staff. Weak leaders simply cannot support strong growth. When I meet with senior leadership teams across the country, they unanimously acknowledge the importance of building the leaders in their organizations. However, many struggle to accomplish it.

Every aspect of your plan is important, but perhaps the most critical section is your leadership team. After all, every other section is carried out by you and the leaders on your team. As the old saying goes, "People truly are your greatest assets." Building them up as leaders might provide your organization with the only real competitive advantage in business.

But most organizations neglect tapping into the true potential of their team. Constrained by antiquated management processes and a dismal culture, most leaders merely uphold out-of-touch policies, procedures, and "best practices." They fail to deliver the results that are possible because they never "practice" the craft of leadership.

Anyone can call themselves an expert marksman by showing up at the rifle range, wearing the appropriate attire, and brandishing a weapon. While you might appear to be a rifleman, looks only go so far. Eventually, people will evaluate you on your results. As a U.S. Marine, being proficient with our weapons required intense focus, dedication, and countless hours of practice.

If we failed to practice our craft, we would fail to produce the desired results. Just showing up in our camouflage uniforms was not good enough when the target was in sight. Many leaders show up and look the part. But unless they practice leadership, on a regular basis, their aim will be off and they will completely miss the target – every time.

People are not born as leaders. That way of thinking has long since passed. Like all things, leadership is a learned behavior. It can and should be trained on all levels in an organization. Once reserved for the select few who hold those positions, leadership development benefits the entire team.

I recently trained over 100 people at the annual workshop for the National Association of Health Unit Coordinators. Representatives from all over the country attended my session. While most were not in a leadership position, I was asked to train them on the benefits of applying leadership skills to their current positions.

I discussed communication, goal-setting, and the 14 Leadership Traits of the Marine Corps. The feedback was overwhelmingly positive. Leadership development, to people who were not in leadership roles, empowered them far more than training. They focused on becoming better team players, helping to build stronger cultures, and achieving greater results.

Exceeding possibilities is one of the elite purpose of all leaders, so it is in your best interest to develop the leadership skills of those around you. Building leaders will help you to achieve results and lift your entire team to new levels of professionalism. To effectively practice leadership and build all leaders on your team, focus on three key areas.

**How to Effectively Practice Leadership and Build Leaders:**

1. Identify Leadership Potential
2. Create Leadership Activities
3. Transfer Leadership Authority

In addition to the intense focus placed on Marines to become proficient with their weapons, their combat skills, and their other occupational specialties, Marines consistently practice leadership. Building up leaders within the ranks of the Corps is not something that might happen, rather it is something that demands the highest level of attention.

## Identify Leadership Potential

Leadership does not have to be a lonely position. Identify and develop current managers and high-performing team members to competently share your responsibilities as a leader. Identifying someone as a possible leader is one of the greatest compliments you can give.

As a leader of leaders, I constantly kept my eyes and ears open to the signs of future leadership. I took opportunities to talk to my staff, assessing their desire to rise up within our organization and contribute to the success of our plan. Within your ranks, identify each current leader and employee who possesses the leadership skills, or the raw potential, to make a greater impact within your organization.

Acknowledging the leadership potential within your team serves many purposes. In addition to allowing for internal growth, it simultaneously guards against unnecessary turnover. It also brings forth more promotions, and fosters an environment of dedication and loyalty.

From a fiscal perspective, it is often less expensive to retain and develop your own talent, rather than hiring from other sources. If your team feels leaders are only hired from outside of your organization, they might look outside of your organization for new opportunities. Allow your team to see opportunities for growth within your company.

During our push for 300 percent growth, the vast majority of our leadership team started their journey with us in entry-level positions, including myself. I was given the opportunity to make an impact and I made a sizable one.

What could your team do if you identified their leadership potential and built them up as leaders?

## Create Leadership Activities

Most organizations have people in leadership positions, but offer very few opportunities for them to hone their skills. Athletes must participate in athletic activities to hone their skills. Their coaches provide unlimited opportunities for them to grow as athletes. Strength training, team practices, one-on-one coaching, and scrimmaging against other teams all help to develop stronger skills.

Leaders need to participate in leadership activities to fine-tune their skills. Your goal is to elevate the leaders on your team above their basic duties, and give them a broader set of responsibilities to support the plan for the organization. I created activities that went far beyond training on the philosophies of leadership. Our activities focused on building our leaders; involving them in actual examples of what to do and what not to do.

To develop my leaders, I held specific leadership meetings, providing them with ways to learn, to share, and to grow with their fellow leaders. In addition to setting high standards for their personal performance, I was involved in hands-on training with each of them, taking specific case studies and analyzing ways each leader could improve their results.

We identified communication with other leaders, other team members, and with customers and vendors. We looked at techniques that worked, and did not work. We sought out solutions that would enable each leader to become the epitome of leadership; to be a shining example to the team of what it meant to be a leader in our organization. We taught them how to be the beacon of hope.

Perhaps one of the greatest activities you can orchestrate is the personal interaction among your leaders. Understanding the need to connect my leaders on levels deeper than our job descriptions, we often met off-site for lunches and dinners. We even conducted some of our meetings at unique locations and at unconventional times.

To unveil our updated plan for the third quarter, we called an optional meeting for our leadership team. The location was on the top floor of the Huntley Hotel, in Santa Monica, California. The meeting was set for Friday evening at their restaurant, The Penthouse. The time was set for midnight. Yes, our meeting began as the clock struck twelve.

All ten members of our leadership team enthusiastically attended and participated. We stayed for nearly three hours. While we discussed the plan, we also discussed our deepest personal goals. We learned much more about each other during this unique activity than we had over the past years of working together. A strong bond was created between our leaders. Changing the environment for our activities often provided our greatest moments of leadership growth.

## Transfer Leadership Authority

The authority of a leader provides the boundaries for course-correcting their team members. Like currency, possessing the proper authority allows a leader to fully invest in their team by combining praising, reprimanding, and influencing. Failing to transfer the proper amount of authority creates a "broke" leader, incapable of making the impact necessary to support the organization's plan for growth.

A leader with no authority is nothing more than a team member who stands higher on the corporate ladder. Leadership positions should not be given as status symbols or ways to appease long-term employees. When a leader earns a promotion, the transference of authority must coincide with the new position.

A leadership role is a huge responsibility to fulfill, for the person in the new position as well as the person who provided the opportunity. Unfortunately, most new leaders are not allowed to exercise the full authority of their positions. Existing leaders, who hold onto the reigns of authority, rather than transitioning them to their leaders, often lack the trust needed to make the transfer. That is specifically why leadership must be earned; never given.

By identifying team members with leadership potential and including them in leadership activities, you can successfully transfer specified levels of authority that will allow them to fully support you and your plan. When a leader has little-to-no authority, it sends a negative message to the entire team, completely negating the new leadership position the person had earned.

Invest the necessary time with your leaders to develop them, coach them, and mentor them. Assess their capabilities with small levels of authority, and work together to increase their ability to take on greater challenges.

A leadership promotion is not complete until an understanding of their authority has been clearly established – to the leader and to the team.

## BECOMING A LEADER OF LEADERS

Within my first six months of serving in the Marine Corps, I was promoted from Private to Private First Class. I was now a leader of Marines and still only eighteen years old. To effectively lead at the highest levels, the Marine Corps emphasized extensive leadership training to all of its Marines. The Corps did not offer one single management course. Everything was built upon leadership training.

As your leadership team grows, your focus should be on the personal development of each member of the team. A quick word of advice: do not attempt to manage your leaders. Become a leader of leaders, taking every possible opportunity to strengthen your people.

Leadership development is an ongoing project. As long as you have leaders on your team, your duty as their leader is never finished. Because many leaders struggle with their own skills, they wonder how they can effectively lead other leaders. Having leaders report to me always kept me focused on increasing my own personal performance.

I have always felt that significant results start in an organization when the next wave of leaders rise up to support the senior leadership team. The problem is that most leaders do not identify and develop this important line of leadership.

The next wave of leaders have their fingers on the pulse; they know what does and does not work. They know who works and who does not. They are your liaison to the team, and it is your objective to connect with them, lead them, and teach them how to lead their teams. To become an effective leader of leaders requires you to show up every day with the highest levels of excellence.

**To Become a Leader of Leaders:**

1. Lead by Example

2. Invest the Time

3. Provide the Feedback

Being a leader is an incredibly rewarding journey. But developing other leaders has always been my greatest pleasure.

## Lead by Example

As a leader, all eyes are on you. Your team analyzes your behavior and critiques your performance. As a leader of leaders, everything intensifies. You are under the microscope 24/7. Your actions, patterns, and habits will be duplicated by your team. Leading by example is the best way to ensure that you stay on track, and your people have the proper model to emulate.

Many leaders think the people working for them are already "set in their ways," and do not have the ability to change, to adapt, to improve. Nothing could be farther from the truth. I have seen many old dogs learn new tricks. It's not the limitations of the dog, but rather the limiting belief level of its trainer that minimizes performance.

I have worked with leaders who pointed out the old dinosaurs on their teams, or the top performers who are negative and stuck doing things "the old way." As these leaders were taught how to lead by example and consistently do the right things, even their "problem children" become star students.

Leading by example makes complete sense, but most leaders fail to do it. It is not about being right; it is about doing right. Do not believe for a second that people do not need you as an example. They absolutely do. Your leaders look to you for the right and wrong ways to do things. Make the choice to lead by example, and do the right things.

Set the right example at all times.

## Invest the Time

Many senior leaders feel they do not have the time to develop their leaders. Making the assumption that they will understand how to lead by observation alone is a critical mistake. Take the time to discuss their struggles and their challenges. They certainly will have them. Ignoring them only makes matters worse.

Investing the time with your leaders to discover solutions is time well spent. Slowing down and spending this critical time with your people will help everyone to speed up and achieve greater results.

While leadership meetings are a great way to encourage leaders to share their thoughts among their peers, I have always found that one-on-one time with my staff was worth every minute. In these relaxed, casual settings, I was able to connect on a deeper level with them. Understanding your leaders is necessary. Developing empathy is critical.

I not only listened to their struggles, but I also shared mine. It is not necessary to make your leaders think you are flawless. When they know you are faced with challenges, and understand how you resolve them, a deeper level of respect and development occurs.

Invest the time necessary to discuss the nuances of their environments; their team member personalities, their working relationships with other leaders, and their ideas about the plan for growth. Leaders need an outlet for their thoughts. Being the outlet will pay off for you, for them, and for your entire organization.

## Provide the Feedback

Leaders do not want to fail. Unfortunately, most do not realize they are heading down the wrong path until something goes wrong. Backing up from a mistake can be costly and timely. It can also lead to frustrations among your leaders.

Have you ever watched little kids bowl? No bowler exhibits the raw excitement and energy like these youngsters do as their ball rolls down the lane. How long would that excitement last if their ball consistently went into the gutter? Eventually, they would give up, never experiencing the feeling of knocking down the pins directly in front of them.

Before their skills are sharpened, these young bowlers enjoy the rush of adrenalin as they consistently knock down the pins, with the help of well-placed bumper rails. Your leaders often need your guidance while they are developing their skills. Like the bumper rails on a bowling lane, your regular feedback helps to keep them on target.

Never assume your leaders will eventually strike the pins on their own. Every leader seeks guidance, strategies, and techniques to achieve better results with their team members. Standing by and watching their ball go into the gutter is not an adequate way to lead other leaders. Eventually they will seek out coaching. Be their first option by providing frequent performance evaluations with impactful suggestions for growth.

Meetings should not become negative sessions, reprimanding and focusing on what your leaders are doing wrong. Instead, help them to address current issues and discover new solutions. I have always found it beneficial to discuss their job duties and their leadership responsibilities.

Performance evaluations might not always feel comfortable, but being a leader of leaders is not about staying in your comfort zone. It is about building leaders and providing them with the support they need for success. Frequent evaluations will help you to catch issues early and prevent your leaders from experiencing unnecessary frustrations. Most leaders will not initially ask for help, so you must discover what their needs are until they trust you enough to directly present their challenges to you.

You cannot rush out to build leaders, which is why we did not discuss it until this chapter. The first ten chapters are critical to developing a foundation that will allow you to fulfill this responsibility.

# CHAPTER 12

## BECOME A VISIONARY LEADER

Train Your Staff, but Develop Your Leaders.

You have taken two great steps toward achieving consistently positive results in your organization. Creating your plan, and building your leaders are essential to achieving new levels of success. But deep inside, you know you possess the ability to accomplish more; to exceed expectations. To take your results to unbelievable new levels, you must raise your skills to the level of a visionary leader.

To become a leader at this level, let's explore what defines this exclusive role. For starters, visionary leaders do not fulfill a position, they fulfill a purpose. More than guiding people to a specified location, visionary leaders often create new, uncharted destinations, while simultaneously articulating the path for success. They are the builders of a new environment, unifying people with a shared sense of adventure and achievement.

Tackling the toughest challenges with the highest levels of professionalism and resolve, people have a strong desire to follow visionary leaders. They work with an inspiring passion and boldness, calling forth the best in each member of their team. Visionary leaders teach people how to exceed possibilities.

In many organizations, leadership development focuses only on a few select individuals. With the desire to enhance their leaders' skills, internal training often centers too much around improving procedural responsibilities. Instructing someone how to manage schedules, comply with regulations, and hire and fire in accordance with company policies, does not make for a better leader.

Today, the corporate environment has changed, and more businesses acknowledge the need to raise the bar on the leadership skills of their key team members. But recognizing and implementing are two different concepts. Most organizations do not have a comprehensive leadership development program in place. In fact, I meet with more and more leaders who receive little-to-no guidance regarding their elite purposes as leaders.

To raise the bar, visionary leaders stretch the vision of their team members, helping them to see the once elusive opportunities that lay ahead. Just as training will not fully cultivate a team, it is not sufficient to develop leaders and stretch their vision.

## THE PROBLEM WITH TRAINING LEADERS

To achieve different results with leadership, you will need to embrace different strategies and techniques. While most organizations fail to build leaders, even fewer invest the time necessary to develop their visionary capabilities.

Like a professional athlete, leaders achieve varying levels of competency and success. Being a good swimmer does not mean you can compete in the Olympics. The development of your skills will have a significant impact on the medal you earn, if you even qualify. To be a gold medalist leader, your development program must be more than a how-to of policies and procedures.

Lately, the terms training and development have slowly become synonymous, and nothing could be farther from the truth. Working with countless organizations, I have observed virtually every type of leadership training program in existence. Unfortunately, most of them do not come close to helping to stretch the vision of other leaders. Surveys, charts, and graphs do little to develop the visionary skills of a leader. Worse yet, most training programs are rarely perceived as being beneficial.

Do not get me wrong, training has its purpose and can be an effective tool, especially for improving the job proficiencies of your team members. But developing leaders and promoting visionary leadership will not happen in a classroom setting. Training reaffirms how to, while development instills why to.

According to Forbes, organizations spend around "$130 billion world-wide" on corporate training and "the #1 areas of spending is management and leadership (35%)." Unfortunately, the only consistent benefactor is usually the training industry, not the organization paying for the training, or the leaders who receive it.

Development is an ongoing journey. The destination is progress, improvement, and growth. Training ends, whereas development continues. The biggest problem with training leaders is that most of the "leadership trainers" are not visionary leaders themselves.

The differences between training and development:

| Training | Development |
|---|---|
| Process | People |
| Present | Future |
| Teach | Transform |
| Seeing inside the box | Envisioning outside the box |
| Tests knowledge | Tests understanding |
| Excepted standards | Unexpected potential |
| Status quo | Status grow |
| Indoctrinate | Innovate |
| Leadership position | Leadership purpose |
| Addresses problems | Identifies solutions |
| Acknowledges limits | Exceeds possibilities |

Training is often a one-dimensional, one-directional undertaking that involves someone standing in front of a podium, using a strict agenda of topics to instruct the audience. The vast majority of training sessions fail because they take place within a lackluster environment, and they tend to focus on past failures as signs of what to avoid.

Even the leaders who passionately want to grow and develop their skills usually dread traditional trainings. Because they do not perceive the value, the only things they focus on avoiding are training sessions. These same leaders will enthusiastically participate in the development of their skills, in an environment conducive to growth.

Development is a shared process of discovery for everyone. Multi-dimensional in nature, it provides coaching, mentoring, and guiding. Focusing on real-life examples, leadership development concentrates all efforts on futures needs and current progress. Development does not deal in the avoidance of issues, but rather a proactive approach to uncover new solutions.

The objective of training is to standardize, and to adapt to the status quo through procedures and best practices. Development is different, embracing a "status grow" approach by identifying the unique attributes of each leader. A leader might guide the session, but everyone is encouraged to participate and share his own successes and failures, with the outcome being focused on growth. Visionary communication is paramount. True development sessions occur in uniquely designed environments.

## VISIONARY ECOSYSTEM

If I gave you an object smaller than a marble, and asked you to place it on the ground, do you believe it could grow to over 350 feet high, 26 feet wide, and weigh more than 500 tons? Does that even seem possible? Can something so small achieve such great levels of growth?

Under the right conditions, it can and does happen naturally, along the coast of central California to southern Oregon. About the same size as a tomato seed, the seeds of the Coastal Redwoods grow and mature into trees that stand nearly forty stories tall. For these trees, the environment is paramount for their growth.

Their ecosystem extends no more than fifty miles inland and they rely on the heavy fog of these areas as protection from the sun and drought. Although each tree can produce 100,000 seeds annually, very few take root. While not every seed will rise to its true potential, those closest to the base of other trees stand a greater chance for survival. Every aspect of their environment plays a critical role in their natural development.

Visionary leaders must pay particular attention to their environment and the conditions they create to grow and develop leaders. Committed to achieving higher level results, visionary leaders must create an ecosystem that stretches the vision of all leaders in their organization. Creating an environment to support the growth of your key players is much like building a greenhouse for leadership development.

Most inexperienced leaders tend to view growth only by looking at their financial statements. ROI, profit margins, and bottom-lines are key indicators of monetary success. But if those alone are how you measure leadership development, you are missing the true potential of creating an ecosystem that produces excellent results, consistently and predictably.

Like all environments on our planet, when the conditions are right, great levels of growth will occur. Because leadership development does not happen naturally, visionary leaders create an environment where they can influence and control the conditions impacting their leaders.

I have discovered that leadership will flourish, and often expand beyond the limitations of an organization, if the conditions are right. An ecosystem that supports great growth occurs when you maintain high levels of the Visionary Vowels listed below:

| | |
|---|---|
| **A** | Attitude |
| **E** | Excellence |
| **I** | Initiative |
| **O** | Outcome |
| **U** | Unwavering |

When these five conditions are present and at the right levels, leadership will grow.

**Attitude** – much like the life-giving rays of light from the sun, leaders must operate with an optimistic, positive, upbeat attitude regardless of their circumstances. Attitude, both positive and negative is highly contagious.

**Excellence** – good is not good enough. Just as the natural terrain supports life, the environment that fosters leadership growth must be highly organized, planned, and structured, for success, while also encouraging new levels of high-performance among each leader.

**Initiative** – in nature, survival does not occur by chance. When there is a passive approach to achieving objectives, growth is severely prohibited. Leaders must take initiative, and empower everyone around them to do the same, and to get things done correctly the first time.

**Outcome** – Mother Nature has a purpose for everything in her world. Leaders must have a purpose and an outcome for everything they do, and everything they ask their teams to do. Each action needs to support that purpose, as it relates to the plan of the organization. An outcome provides the nourishment for sustainable growth.

**Unwavering** – survival is not guaranteed. Every living creature possesses an unwavering commitment to stay alive, and they fight for it. Every leader, at every level, must possess an unwavering commitment to growth and development. Fight for the success of your leaders.

Creating a visionary ecosystem will allow every leader, and potential leader, to understand the conditions necessary for growth, and support them at the highest levels. Visionary leaders develop other leaders, in a collaborative environment of trust and respect.

I did not merely create a visionary ecosystem to support the achievement of 300 percent annual revenue growth. I protected and guarded that environment because it provided the conditions necessary to support my leaders, and to help them to grow and develop in accordance with our plan.

## STRETCHING VISION

There's no denying being a U.S. Marine was challenging. As an air traffic controller (ATC), additional levels of stress were certainly added. The lives of pilots and their passengers were on the line every time I put on my headset and communicated detailed instructions to them. As you can imagine, our training was intense.

After graduating from ATC school, I reported to Marine Corps Air Station, Yuma, Arizona. I began working in the control tower, and my training continued on-the-job. Every word I spoke into my headset was under tight scrutiny and analyzed to determine how I could improve.

I learned much from my job experiences in this field, but my training ended on the day I hung up my headset for the last time. My leadership development, however, did not end on August, 23, 1991, when my tour of duty ended. It has been an integral part of my life for over twenty years.

Marine Corps leaders stretched my vision, and not a day goes by I do not tap into the elite leadership skills I learned in the Marine Corps. Visionary leadership has a permanent impact on people. Job training might serve an immediate need, but having your vision stretched will serve a life-long purpose for those who receive it.

To make the final link to becoming a visionary leader, you must stretch the vision of your leaders, ensuring they consistently look for ways to exceed possibilities. The transition to visionary leadership is a great responsibility. It is both intimidating and exhilarating at the same time. Deciding to become a leader who stretches the vision of others will enhance your personal leadership skills.

As you transform the big picture of your organization into reality, focus on three elite actions that uniquely stretch peoples' vision. These actions will allow you to become the catalyst for positive changes in your organization and will help to forge an amazing future for everyone on your team.

**Vision Stretching Actions:**

1. Future thinking

2. Failing forward

3. Adding significance

**Future Thinking** – having vision is an important quality for every leader. Vision is seeing what is ahead; the possibilities in the future. Most leaders are so overwhelmed with the present they never take the time to explore the unknown possibilities of the future.

Visionary leaders constantly engage others in discussions about the results of the future and what is required to attain them. Future thinking allows leaders to develop a better understanding of the path that lies ahead. Simply sharing the vision of the organization might not provide sufficient inspiration for each leader.

A visionary leader must stretch the vision of their leaders, influencing them to choose to be a part of the future progress. Future thinking is long term thinking, and long-term thinking helps with leadership retention. Leaders are more inclined to stay, and be active with an organization when they understand the direction they are headed.

Many leaders might not be able to initially see the final picture in full clarity. Your continued efforts to stretch their vision will improve their sight and their belief in a positive future. Visionary leaders focus on the results of the future in order to strengthen the actions taken in the present.

Future thinking encourages leaders to focus on where they are headed rather than where they have been. They begin to imagine the opportunities of tomorrow rather than dwelling on the problems of yesterday.

**Failing Forward** – failing and leadership should never be spoken in the same sentence, right? Success might very well be the opposite of failure, but it is impossible to achieve extraordinary results without the valuable lessons learned through the experiences of failing.

Vision can only be transformed into reality when actions are taken. But too many leaders are hesitant to move forward due to the fear of failing. Understandably so, some failures might cost them their job. But visionary leaders create a balance in their ecosystem, removing fear from their leaders by creating an environment where failures are perceived as opportunities to improve; opportunities to discover new ways to exceed possibilities.

Visionary leadership is not achieved by getting everything right, but rather discovering ways of not doing it wrong. By stretching the vision of your leaders, they will transform failures into opportunities for growth, and will be empowered to take the risks necessary for unparalleled results.

Visionary leaders are optimistic, seeing an opportunity in everything that occurs in their ecosystem. They look for areas of growth in every situation, and in every failure. They convey an understanding among all leaders that failing is only considered a failure when it stops someone from trying again. All great leaders have suffered failures. Visionary leaders teach their people how to seek the valuable lessons contained in every issue, problem, or setback.

**Leadership Link** Never experience "failures." Instead, write them off as "learning experiences." Every failure can improve skills and increase confidence.

**Adding Significance** – leading an organization can often be a nearly thankless job, especially for leaders who fail to connect with people on a deeper level than merely job performance. The most important thing we do by stretching people's vision is adding significance to their lives; making an impact in who they are, not just what they do.

The greatest attributes of becoming a visionary leader is not developing new products and services, nor is it expanding into new markets. It is adding significance to the lives of others. Visionary leaders inspire other leaders because they are inspired themselves. By sharing the possibilities of creating an exciting future for their organization, visionary leaders encourage people to look for the exciting enhancements that await them in their personal lives.

Visionary leaders teach leaders to view themselves as victors over their circumstances, rather than being victims of their circumstances. This is a significant perception anyone can apply to their personal lives, not just their professional ones.

When leaders grow in an environment that adds significance to their lives, they stop criticizing and finger-pointing when things go wrong. They begin to work with others to seek out solutions. As those solutions are discovered, visionary leaders refuse credit, giving it to others, adding significance to their lives.

## THE LEADERSHIP CONNECTION

Leaders are only limited by their own vision. Creating an ecosystem that adds significance allows you to stretch their vision and improve their ability to grow. Stretching the vision of others does not happen by chance, nor is it the side effect of merely being a good leader. To stretch someone's vision; to provide them with a new perspective on a bright future, you must be a visionary leader.

In the quest for greater results, most leaders attempt to differentiate their organization from the competition. While there is merit to this strategy, visionary leaders take a different approach, striving to differentiate their leaders from the leaders of their competitors. Stretching the vision of your people will increase the likelihood of consistent growth and development. As a visionary leader, you are the catalyst for a dynamic paradigm shift – one that will create a new and exciting destination. To arrive there, develop a team of leaders; a team of visionary leaders. You have the ability to create an environment that improves performance, increases results, and impacts the lives of everyone who comes into contact with this new wave of leadership.

Be the leader who makes The LEADERSHIP Connection!

# ACKNOWLEDGMENTS

## My Deepest Gratitude

To my wife, Gina. Your constant support has not only encouraged me to complete this book, but has inspired me to become a better leader.

To my son, Brandyn. Your desire and artistic skills created the amazing "links" which grace the inside of this book, truly bringing it to life.

To my son, Jacob. Your belief in me has always been a driving force in my life.

To my daughter, Erika. Your hard work at my office helped me to stay on track with this book.

# ABOUT THE AUTHOR

## ERIK THERWANGER

Erik Therwanger began his unique career by serving in the U.S. Marine Corps. Leadership, honor, and integrity did not end after his four year tour of duty; they became the foundation of his life, both personally and professionally.

After receiving the news that his wife had been diagnosed with cancer, Erik left his job in the entertainment industry, became her caregiver, and started his new career in sales. With no formal training, he began selling financial services. Relying on the strategies and techniques he learned as a Marine, he quickly became a top producer, recruiter, and trainer.

Erik's passion for helping others led to the creation of Think GREAT®. He successfully blends his leadership skills, his unparalleled ability to inspire and develop teams, and his wide array of sales experience, to provide practical solutions for individuals and organizations.

Sharing his personal story and elite strategies, Erik inspires audiences to strive for new levels of greatness. His interactive and powerful workshops highlight his step–by–step process for increasing results: The Trifecta of Growth™. Erik delivers a compelling message that leaves a lasting impact in organizations, creating the necessary momentum to develop strong leaders, build visionary teams, and elevate sales results.

As the author of the Think GREAT® Collection, Erik has combined his challenging life experiences with his goal–setting techniques, to provide proven strategies to enhance the lives of others.

As part of his greater purpose, Erik dedicates time to helping in the fight against cancer by volunteering with the Relay For Life. Erik is also a member of the Marine Corps League and Beyond the Yellow Ribbon, participating in events to support our nation's veterans and their families.

# Think**GREAT**®

## WWW.THINKGREAT90.COM

Please visit our website for additional information to help you and your organization achieve greater results:

- Powerful products
- Inspirational seminars
- Interactive tools
- Events and appearances with Erik Therwanger
- Register for the FREE Great Thought of the Week
- News, blog, and forum

For additional information, please visit
http://www.thinkgreat90.com

More life-changing books in the Think GREAT® Collection:

- The GOAL Formula

- 3–D Sales

- The SCALE Factor

- Goal Planning Strategy (G*P*S*) Workbook